REVISE EDEXCEL GCSE
Science

REVISION GUIDE

Foundation

Series Consultant: Harry Smith

Series Editor: Penny Johnson

Authors: Penny Johnson, Sue Kearsey, Damian Riddle

A note from the publisher

In order to ensure that this resource offers high-quality support for the associated Pearson qualification, it has been through a review process by the awarding body. This process confirms that this resource fully covers the teaching and learning content of the specification or part of a specification at which it is aimed. It also confirms that it demonstrates an appropriate balance between the development of subject skills, knowledge and understanding, in addition to preparation for assessment.

Endorsement does not cover any guidance on assessment activities or processes (e.g. practice questions or advice on how to answer assessment questions), included in the resource nor does it prescribe any particular approach to the teaching or delivery of a related course.

While the publishers have made every attempt to ensure that advice on the qualification and its assessment is accurate, the official specification and associated assessment guidance materials are the only authoritative source of information and should always be referred to for definitive guidance.

Pearson examiners have not contributed to any sections in this resource relevant to examination papers for which they have responsibility.

Examiners will not use endorsed resources as a source of material for any assessment set by Pearson.

Endorsement of a resource does not mean that the resource is required to achieve this Pearson qualification, nor does it mean that it is the only suitable material available to support the qualification, and any resource lists produced by the awarding body shall include this and other appropriate resources.

For the full range of Pearson revision titles across GCSE, BTEC and AS/A Level visit:
www.pearsonschools.co.uk/revise

ALWAYS LEARNING

PEARSON

Contents

A small bit of small print

Edexcel publishes Sample Assessment Material and the Specification on its website. This is the official content and this book should be used in conjunction with it. The questions in *Now try this* have been written to help you practise every topic in the book. Remember: the real exam questions may not look like this.

Target grade ranges
Target grade ranges are quoted in this book for some of the questions. Students targeting this grade range should be aiming to get most of the marks available. Students targeting a higher grade should be aiming to get all of the marks available.

1-to-1 page match with the Core Foundation Workbook ISBN 978-1-446-902608

Classification

Classification groups

Classification means grouping things by their features or characteristics. The more characteristics that are used to group similar organisms together, the more reliable is the classification.

Small groups that are similar can be grouped into larger groups. Kingdoms are the largest groups in classifying organisms, and species are the smallest.

A mnemonic like this can help you remember the groups in the right order: **K**eep **P**ond **C**lean **O**r **F**rogs **G**et **S**ick.

Kingdom	Phylum	Class	Order	Family	Genus	Species
Group of similar phyla e.g. Animalia	Group of similar classes e.g. Chordata	Group of similar orders e.g. Mammalia	Group of similar families e.g. Carnivora	Group of similar genera e.g. Canidae (dog family)	Group of similar species e.g. Canis	Organisms that have most characteristics in common e.g. *Canis lupus* (domesticated dog)

The five kingdoms of organisms

1 Animalia (animals)
- multicellular (body made of many cells)
- have no cell walls
- no chlorophyll in cells
- feed heterotrophically (eat other organisms)

3 Fungi
- multicellular
- have cell walls
- no chlorophyll
- feed saprophytically (digest food outside the body)

2 Plantae (plants)
- multicellular
- have cell walls
- have chlorophyll
- feed autotrophically (make own food)

4 Protoctista
- mostly unicellular (body is a single cell)
- nucleus in cell

5 Prokaryotae (mostly bacteria)
- unicellular
- no nucleus in cell

Worked example

Viruses are not classified in a kingdom. Explain why.

They are not classified because most scientists think that viruses are not living organisms. This is because:
- They have to use other cells to reproduce.
- They show no other life processes (for example, growth).

Now try this

1. List the seven classification groups of organisms in order, starting with the largest. **(1 mark)**

   target **G-D**

2. Describe how you would tell the difference between the following:

   (a) a plant and a fungus **(2 marks)**

   (b) a protoctist and a prokaryote (bacterium). **(2 marks)**

Vertebrates and invertebrates

The phylum Chordata contains animals that have a supporting rod running the length of their body. Many animals in the Chordata are vertebrates (animals with backbones).

Vertebrate groups

Scientists sort vertebrates into five main groups.

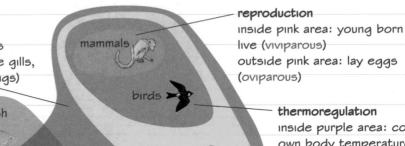

oxygen absorbtion
inside blue area: use gills
inside green area: use lungs
(note: young amphibians use gills, but adult amphibians use lungs)

fertilisation
inside yellow area:
inside female's body (internal)
outside yellow area:
outside female's body (external)

reproduction
inside pink area: young born live (viviparous)
outside pink area: lay eggs (oviparous)

thermoregulation
inside purple area: control own body temperature (homeotherm)
outside purple area: body temperature varies with environment temperature (poikilotherm)

Worked example

Bats and birds are vertebrates with wings, but they are classified in different vertebrate groups. Use these examples to help explain why it is sometimes difficult to classify vertebrates.

Bats and birds both have wings and can fly. Other characteristics are very different so they should be classified in different groups. Bats are mammals because they give birth to live young. Birds lay hard-shelled eggs.

Organisms that live in similar ways often have similar characteristics as a result of adaptation to their environment. It can be easy to confuse these characteristics with those shared as a result of evolution.

Now try this

target
G–D

1. Name the five main groups of vertebrates.   **(5 marks)**

2. Match each word to its correct definition.

	Definitions
oviparous	controlled body temperature
viviparous	lays eggs
poikilotherm	live births
homeotherm	varying body temperature

(4 marks)

Species

Defining 'species'

Scientists define a species as a group of organisms that can breed with each other and produce fertile offspring. Fertile means that the offspring can produce their own offspring when they are adults. A few species can interbreed and produce hybrid offspring, but usually these hybrids are sterile, which means they cannot produce offspring of their own.

This definition of a species can cause problems.

Some organisms from closely related species can interbreed and produce hybrid offspring that *are* fertile.	For example, tigers have been bred with lions in zoos to produce fertile hybrids called tigons or ligers.
Some organisms produce offspring from parts of their body (plants and fungi) or by dividing in two (bacteria and protoctists).	If we never see two organisms breeding together, we cannot be sure if they are of the same species or not.

Worked example

All these animals belong to the same species, *Canis lupus* (domesticated dog). Use the pictures to help you explain why it can be difficult to classify organisms into species.

Individuals in a species can show a lot of variation. This makes it difficult to classify them because we rely on what organisms look like to help us classify them.

How scientists work

When scientists make a new discovery, such as finding a new species, they tell other scientists by:

- writing a paper and sending it to a scientific journal – before the paper is accepted by the journal it is checked by other scientists to make sure it is good enough to be published, and this check is called peer review

- presenting their discovery to other scientists at scientific conferences.

Sharing new discoveries makes it possible for other scientists to check that the findings are reliable.

Variation is the difference in characteristics between organisms.

Now try this

1. State one way that scientists tell everyone about a new discovery. **(1 mark)**

2. State two problems with classifying a group of organisms as a species. **(2 marks)**

3. Describe what we mean by variation in a species. **(1 mark)**

Variation

When we find an organism that we don't know, we can use a key to help identify what species it is.

Worked example

Use the key for big cats to identify this animal.

1	Has no spots?	go to 2
	Has a spotted coat?	go to 4
2	Has stripes?	tiger
	Has no stripes?	go to 3
3	Has ring of dark fur round nose and mouth?	puma
	Has no ring of dark fur?	lion
4	Has simple spots of same size all over?	cheetah
	Has rosettes (patterns of spots)?	go to 5
5	Rosettes have small dots inside?	jaguar
	Rosettes have no dots inside?	leopard

Choose the statement that matches the organism most closely.

Your choice might give you an instruction to follow.

Your choice might tell you what the organism is.

The animal has a spotted coat (1→4), has patterns of spots (4→5), and has small dots inside the rosettes. So it is a jaguar.

Constructing a key

Start by separating the organisms into groups using obvious characteristics. The key above starts by separating the big cats into those with spots and those without spots. Continue separating each group into smaller groups using obvious characteristics until you have only one organism in each group.

A diagram like this can help you construct your key.

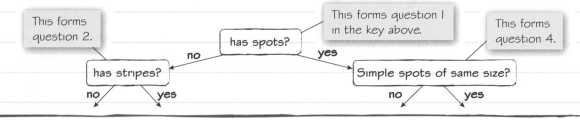

This forms question 2.

This forms question 1 in the key above.

This forms question 4.

has spots?

no   yes

has stripes?

no   yes

Simple spots of same size?

no   yes

Now try this

target G-E

1. Explain what an identification key is used for. **(1 mark)**

target D-C

2. Construct a key to identify these four animals. **(4 marks)**

Reasons for variety

Different species are adapted to living in different environments. Organisms that live in extreme environments need special adaptations.

| Deep-sea hydrothermal vent organisms | | Polar organisms | |
Environment	Adaptations	Environment	Adaptations
little light	no eyes	white snow and ice	white fur for camouflage
extremely hot water	sense organs that detect dangerously high temperatures	very cold in winter	to reduce the amount of heat leaving the body organisms may have: • thick fur • extra fat below skin • bulky body • small ears
acidic water, at high pressure and full of minerals	soft parts strengthened by iron scales		
low oxygen concentration in water	haemoglobin to help take oxygen from water	slippery ice	wide feet with rough soles to help grip the ice

Worked example

Before the Antarctic winter begins, Emperor penguins build up a thick layer of fat beneath their skin. Explain how this helps them survive.

The Antarctic winter is very cold. A thick layer of fat acts as insulation against the cold air and prevents the inside of the penguin's body losing too much heat.

EXAM ALERT!

In an exam answer be clear about which environmental conditions an organism is adapted to, and how each characteristic helps them to survive those conditions.

Students have struggled with exam questions similar to this - **be prepared!**   ResultsPlus

Types of variation

Discontinuous variation

Characteristics controlled by genes (genetic variation), e.g. blood group, gender.

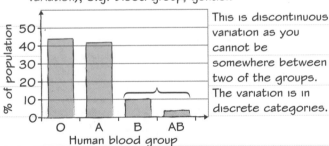

This is discontinuous variation as you cannot be somewhere between two of the groups. The variation is in discrete categories.

Continuous variation

Acquired characteristics controlled by genes and the environment (environmental variation), e.g. height, weight.

This is continuous variation because the characteristic can fall anywhere between the values shown on the axis.

The bell shape of a graph showing continuous variation is called a normal distribution curve.

Now try this

target G-E

1. Name two extreme environmental conditions that occur near deep-sea hydrothermal vents.   **(2 marks)**

2. Choose the right words to make these sentences correct.

   (a) When a characteristic only occurs in distinct forms, it shows *continuous/discontinuous* variation.   **(1 mark)**

target G-D

   (b) Human blood group is an example of *continuous/discontinuous* variation.   **(1 mark)**

   (c) Discontinuous variation is caused *by genes only/by genes and the environment*.   **(1 mark)**

3. Arctic foxes have thick fur and are white in winter. Explain how these characteristics are adaptations to the environment.   **(2 marks)**

target F-C

Evolution

Natural selection

Individuals of a species show variation. This can mean that some individuals will be better able to survive in their environment and produce more healthy offspring than others. This is natural selection, where the environment (including climate and other organisms) selects which individuals pass on their genes to the next generation.

Adults usually produce more young than the environment can support when they are adults (overproduction). This produces a 'struggle for existence' by the young.

→ Some individuals have inherited advantageous variations in characteristics that are better adapted to the environment. These individuals will have a better chance of survival to adulthood.

→ Individuals with advantageous variations will pass their genes on to their young. The young may inherit the advantageous variations.

→ More individuals will have these advantageous variations in the next generation.

Individuals with variations that are not as well adapted to the environment will be less likely to survive.

→ These individuals will not produce young.

Evolution

Charles Darwin (1809–1882) suggested that, if the environment changes, then natural selection will result in the characteristics of a species changing gradually from generation to generation. This change is called evolution.

Environment changes (e.g. gets colder). → Different variations help individuals to survive and produce more young (e.g. thicker fur/more fat). → Characteristics of species gradually change from generation to generation (e.g. all individuals have thicker fur/more fat).

Recent studies of DNA show that organisms that have the most similar DNA are the most closely related. This is predicted by Darwin's theory.

Worked example

Write labels for the diagrams to explain how antibiotic resistance in a bacterial population provides evidence for evolution by natural selection.

Before use of antibiotic

Straight after use of antibiotic

Much later after use of antibiotic

Key
Each dot is a colony containing many bacteria.
↓ Increasing resistance to antibiotic

1 There is variation in level of resistance to the antibiotic in different bacteria.

2 When the antibiotic is used, only the most resistant bacteria survive. The rest die.

3 The surviving bacteria produce new bacteria that are all very resistant to the antibiotic. So antibiotic resistance has evolved.

Now try this

1. Give two sources of recent evidence for Darwin's theory of evolution by natural selection. **(2 marks)**

2. Define these terms: **(a)** natural selection, **(b)** evolution. **(2 marks)**

3. One way of preventing the evolution of antibiotic-resistant bacteria could be to limit the use antibiotics. Explain why. **(2 marks)**

target G-D

target F-C

target D-C

Genes

Inside a cell

Most cells contain a nucleus in which there are chromosomes.

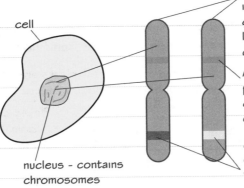

cell

nucleus - contains chromosomes

There are two copies of each chromosome in body cells – each copy has the same genes in the same order along its length (except chromosomes that determine sex).

A gene is a short piece of DNA at a particular point on a chromosome – a gene codes for a characteristic, e.g. eye colour.

A gene may come in different forms, called alleles, that produce different variations of the characteristic, e.g. different eye colours.

Alleles

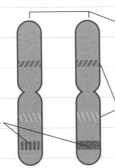

different alleles of the same gene – the person is heterozygous for this gene

chromosomes of the same type are the same size and have the same genes in the same order

these genes have the same allele on both chromosomes – the person is homozygous for these genes

Remember that alleles are alternative forms of the same gene.

Genetic definitions

The alleles for a characteristic can be represented with letters, as shown in this example. Rabbits have different coat colours. The allele for brown colour (B) is dominant over the allele for black colour (b). The table shows all the possible genotypes and phenotypes for these alleles.

Genotype shows the alleles (forms of the genes) in the individual. Remember that each body cell has two genes for each characteristic – so either two alleles that are the same or two that are different.

Phenotype means the characteristics that are produced, including what the individual looks like.

Genotype	Phenotype
BB	brown coat
Bb	brown coat
bb	black coat

The effect of the dominant allele will show when at least one copy is present in the genotype.

A dominant allele is not bigger or stronger than a recessive allele. It is dominant because you see its effect on the characteristic even if you only have one copy of it.

The effect of the recessive allele will only show when two copies are present in the genotype.

target G-D

target D-C

1. Write down the meaning of these words:
   (a) allele   **(1 mark)**   (b) gene.   **(1 mark)**

2. A pea plant has a recessive allele for white flower colour and a dominant allele for purple flower colour.
   (a) Identify if the plant is homozygous or heterozygous for flower colour, and explain your answer.   **(2 marks)**
   (b) State whether the plant will have purple or white flowers. Explain your answer.   **(2 marks)**

Explaining inheritance

Monohybrid inheritance

Sometimes a characteristic is controlled by a single gene. This is called monohybrid inheritance. We can use a genetic diagram to help us understand how alleles are inherited.

Body cells contain two alleles for each gene. Both parent plants are heterozygous – they have one allele for purple flower colour and one allele for white flower colour.

parent plants | R r | R r | Purple colour is dominant (R). White colour is recessive (r).

pollen grains | egg cells

different possible gametes | R | r | R | r | Half the gametes contain one allele. The other half contain the other allele.

possible combinations

genotype — RR Rr Rr Rr
phenotype —

Worked example

Green seed pod (G) is dominant to yellow seed pod (g). Complete the Punnett square to show the possible offspring for plants heterozygous for seed pod colour, and calculate the (a) ratio, (b) probability and (c) percentage of possible offspring genotypes and phenotypes.

parent gametes	parent genotype Gg	
	G	g
parent genotype Gg G	GG green	Gg green
g	Gg green	gg yellow

(a) Genotype 1 GG : 2 Gg : 1gg
   Phenotype 3 green : 1 yellow

(b) Genotype 1/4 (1 out of 4) GG, 2/4 (1/2) Gg, and 1/4 gg
   Phenotype 3/4 green and 1/4 yellow

(c) Genotype 25% GG, 50% Gg, 25% gg
   Phenotype 75% green and 25% yellow

A Punnett square is a different way of showing the same information about how genotype is inherited and what effect this has on the phenotype.

Genetic diagrams and Punnett squares only show *possible* offspring, not the *actual* offspring from these parents.

EXAM ALERT!

Take great care to complete the square correctly. Using the wrong letters will mean that you won't get all the marks available.

Students have struggled with exam questions similar to this - **be prepared!**

ResultsPlus

Now try this

1. Coat colour is inherited in rabbits by one gene. The dominant allele for this gene (B) gives a brown coat. The recessive allele (b) gives a black coat.
   (a) Write down the genotype and phenotype for a rabbit that is heterozygous for coat colour. **(2 marks)**
   (b) Draw a Punnett square to show the possible offspring from two heterozygous parents. **(2 marks)**
   (c) Write down the ratios of possible genotypes and phenotypes of the offspring. **(2 marks)**

Genetic disorders

Some genes have faulty alleles that cause health problems. These are genetic disorders.

Sickle cell disease

A recessive allele of the haemoglobin gene causes red blood cells to become sickle-shaped when blood oxygen concentration is low. People with two copies of this allele may:

- become short of breath and get tired easily
- have reduced blood flow if red blood cells block a blood vessel, which may cause damage to body tissues, heart attack, stroke or even death.

Cystic fibrosis

Worked example

Describe the symptoms of cystic fibrosis.

Mucus that lines tubes in the lungs and other parts of the body is much thicker and stickier than normal. This can:
- lead to many infections of the lungs
- prevent enzymes getting into the digestive system to break down food, which can lead to weight loss.

Family pedigrees

A family pedigree is a diagram that shows the inheritance of a characteristic in a family. Pedigree analysis can help us predict the chance that someone has inherited a particular allele.

Ethan inherited his alleles from Arun and Beth. But they don't have the disease, so they must both be carriers (have one copy of the faulty allele).

Three generations are shown in this pedigree. Arun and Beth are the oldest generation.

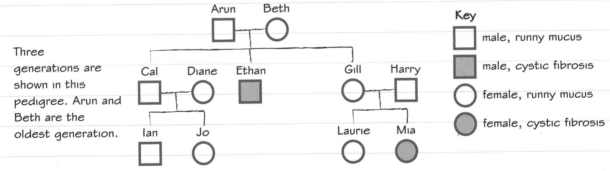

Ethan and Mia must have two copies of the recessive allele, as they have the disease.

Now try this

1. (a) Name one genetic disorder. **(1 mark)**
   (b) Describe two symptoms of the genetic disorder you named in part (a). **(2 marks)**

2. What is a family pedigree? **(2 marks)**

3. (a) In the family pedigree shown above, identify two people, other than Arun and Beth, who are definitely carriers for cystic fibrosis. **(1 mark)**
   (b) Explain your answer to part (a). **(2 marks)**

Biology extended writing 1

To answer an extended writing question successfully you need to:
- ✓ use your scientific knowledge to answer the question
- ✓ organise your answer so that it is logical and well ordered
- ✓ use full sentences in your writing and make sure that your spelling, punctuation and grammar are correct.

Worked example

Question 1

The oystercatcher is a bird. It lives on the sea shore and walks across mud flats, where it finds its food under the surface of the mud. It eats oysters, which are a kind of shellfish.
It has a long, strong beak; long legs, wide feet and dark, plain feathers.
Describe how the oystercatcher has adapted to live in its environment. **(6 marks)**

Sample answer 1

The bird has a very long beak. It can use its beak to dig into the mud to find food. The strong beak means it can break open the shells of oysters and other shellfish that it catches.

This is a basic answer. It mostly gives information that is already in the question – oystercatchers have long beaks and oystercatchers find food under the surface of the mud. However, it does add a little extra information – the idea that the beak can be used to probe under the mud, and that it is strong enough to open shells. To improve, the answer would need to describe some other adaptations in the oystercatcher.

Sample answer 2

The oystercatcher has to be able to walk across mud flats without sinking, and so its wide feet help by spreading its weight. The long legs also help the oystercatcher to wade out into shallow water, so that it can find food in different areas. The dull feathers of the bird mean that it blends into the muddy areas where it feeds, so that it is less obvious to predators. The long, strong beak allows the oystercatcher to dig into the mud to find shells, and then to open them.

This is an excellent answer and is very detailed. It describes how each of the adaptations mentioned in the question is used by the oystercatcher to survive in its environment. The answer is well structured, the information is presented clearly and it uses good scientific terminology (such as 'predators').

Now try this

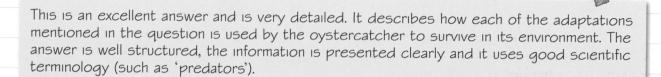

1. Explain how the polar bear is able to survive in the very cold climate at the North Pole. **(6 marks)**

Biology extended writing 2

Worked example

Question 1

Sickle cell disease is a **recessive** genetic disorder (see page 11) in which haemoglobin can change under some conditions and makes red blood cells which are sickle shaped. The red blood cells can then become stuck in capillaries and this can cause damage to body tissues.

Two parents are both **heterozygous** for the sickle cell allele.

Use the information provided by the bold words to explain the probability that these parents will have a child with sickle cell disease.   **(6 marks)**

Sample answer 1

A recessive condition means that you have to have two copies of the allele in order to get it. So, if the parents both pass on the recessive allele for sickle cell disease, their child will have the condition. Because they are heterozygous, they both have the allele so their child will have sickle cell disease.

This is a basic answer. The student understands what is meant by a recessive condition. However, they do not seem to understand what heterozygous means. The answer given suggests that the probability of the child having sickle cell disease is 100%, which is not correct. To improve the answer, it would help to describe 'heterozygous' more clearly and to draw a Punnett square (see page 10) to help you to work out and explain the probability.

Sample answer 2

The parents are heterozygous – this means that they each have a copy of the allele which means no sickle cell disease (D) and a copy of the allele responsible for sickle cell disease (d).

Sickle cell disease is a recessive condition, so the genotype of people with the disease will be dd. In other words, the child would have to inherit the sickle cell allele (d) from both parents in order to develop the disease.

		Mother Dd	
		Gametes	
		D	d
	Gametes		
Father	D	DD	Dd
Dd			
	d	dD	dd

The probability of these parents having a child with the disease is therefore 1 in 4.

This is an excellent answer. The student understands the words in bold in the question, and has given clear definitions. They have chosen clear letters (D and d) to illustrate the dominant and recessive alleles, and they have also shown a genetic cross between these parents. The final answer is correct. This answer also uses better scientific language than Sample Answer 1 (for example, 'inherit' is better than 'get' when talking about passing the alleles on).

Now try this

1. Discuss the structure and role of chromosomes.   **(6 marks)**

Homeostasis

Some conditions in the body need to be maintained at a constant level. This process of keeping the inside of the body stable is known as homeostasis. Keeping conditions stable helps the body to work well.

Osmoregulation

Too much or too little water in the body can cause harm. Osmoregulation controls how much water is lost in urine. This helps to control the amount of water in the body.

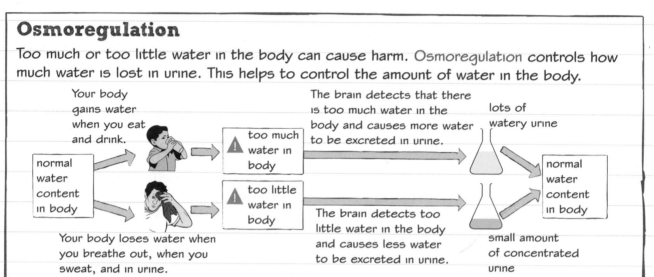

Blood glucose regulation

Blood glucose regulation makes sure that the concentration of glucose in the blood stays within a small range of values. Too little glucose in the blood is harmful, because glucose is needed by cells for respiration. Too much glucose in the blood is also harmful. Mechanisms in the body control the amount of glucose in the blood.

Worked example

Use the graph to help you explain why blood glucose regulation is an example of homeostasis.

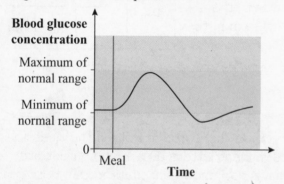

Blood glucose rises after a meal because glucose is absorbed into the blood from the small intestine. Mechanisms in the body cause glucose to be taken out of the blood so that it doesn't get too high. When the glucose levels fall too low, mechanisms cause some glucose to be released back into the blood. This keeps blood glucose within safe limits, which is called homeostasis.

Now try this

target **G-D**

1. Fill in the correct words to complete the sentence.
   Homeostasis means keeping conditions
   .... the body ....
   (2 marks)

2. Describe how osmoregulation controls the water content of the body. **(2 marks)**

target **F-D**

3. Explain why blood glucose concentration changes after a meal. **(2 marks)**

target **F-C**

Thermoregulation

The temperature inside your body is kept steady at around 37 °C by thermoregulation.

Control of thermoregulation

The hypothalamus is a small part of the brain that monitors body temperature by measuring blood temperature. The hypothalamus also receives information about the temperature of the environment from nerve endings deep in the skin – in the dermis.

The hypothalamus controls responses if the body gets too hot or too cold.

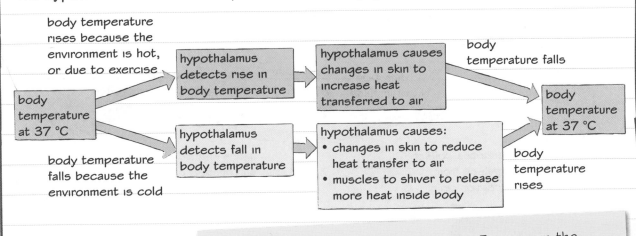

Enzymes control reactions inside cells. Enzymes in the main organs (e.g. heart, liver, brain) are most active at around 37 °C. If the body gets too hot or too cold, the enzymes don't work so well and you can quickly become ill.

Worked example

Explain how the skin helps to regulate body temperature:
(a) When body temperature is too low.
(b) When body temperature is too high.

(a) • Body hair is raised when the erector muscles contract.
• Sebaceous glands produce oil that repel water from skin.

• Blood flow is reduced near the skin surface.
These changes reduce heat transfer to the surroundings.

(b) • Sweat gland produces sweat that evaporates from skin surface.
• Blood flow is increased near skin surface.
These changes increase heat transfer to the surroundings.

Now try this

target
G-D

1. Identify which of these conditions in the body is controlled by thermoregulation:
   (a) water **(b)** temperature
   (c) blood glucose concentration. **(1 mark)**

2. Write down the name of the part of the brain that monitors body temperature.
   (1 mark)

target
E-C

3. Draw labelled diagrams to show how changes in the skin:
   (a) increase heat transfer to the air when the body is too hot **(1 mark)**
   (b) reduce heat transfer to the air when the body is too cold. **(1 mark)**

Sensitivity

The human nervous system includes...

- the central nervous system – brain and spinal cord ◄
- the sense organs, such as the eyes and ears, contain receptors, which detect a change in the environment, called a stimulus, and produce an electrical impulse
- the nerves that join the central nervous system to the sense organs and effector organs. These are made up of bundles of nerve cells, or neurones.

> Watch out! Don't confuse the *spine*, which is the bony structure in your back, with the *spinal cord*, which is made of nerves. The spinal cord lies inside the spine for protection.

Neurone structure

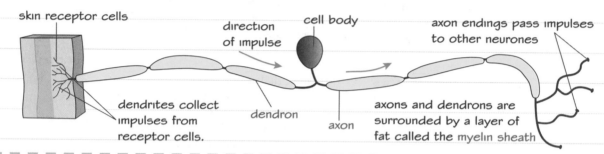

skin receptor cells

direction of impulse

cell body

axon endings pass impulses to other neurones

dendrites collect impulses from receptor cells.

dendron

axon

axons and dendrons are surrounded by a layer of fat called the myelin sheath

Worked example

Explain how the structure of dendrons and axons is related to their function of carrying nerve impulses.

> Watch out! You will get no marks for writing about nerves carrying messages. You should always use the term nerve impulses instead.

The long dendron carries the nerve impulse from receptor cells. The long axon carries the nerve impulse to other neurones. The fatty myelin sheath insulates the neurone, so that the electrical impulse is carried quickly to the end of the axon.

Different types of neurone

	Sensory neurone	Relay neurone	Motor neurone
Found in:	nerves	central nervous system neurones	nerves
Structure:	long dendron and long axon	many short branches	long axon
Function:	carries impulses from receptors to central nervous system	links sensory, motor and other relay neurones	carries impulses from central nervous system to effector organs

Now try this

target
G-D

target
F-D

1. Name the two structures that make up the central nervous system. **(2 marks)**

2. (a) Describe the function of a sensory neurone. **(1 mark)**

(b) Describe the function of a motor neurone. **(1 mark)**

(c) Identify the part of the nervous system that is mainly made from relay neurones. **(1 mark)**

Responding to stimuli

Some parts of the skin are more sensitive than others. This can be tested by touching different parts of the skin with two points and finding out how close the points can be while they are still identified as two points, rather than one point.

Synapses

The point where two neurones meet is called a synapse. There is a small gap between the neurones. The electrical nerve impulse cannot cross this gap, and the impulse is carried by neurotransmitters.

(1) Electrical nerve impulse reaches end of axon.

synapse

(2) Electrical impulse causes chemical neurotransmitter to be released into gap between neurones.

(3) Neurotransmitter causes new electrical impulse in next neurone.

The reflex arc

A reflex arc is the simplest neurone pathway from a receptor cell to an effector organ.

Worked example

The diagram shows a reflex arc.

(a) Identify structures A, B and C in the diagram.

(b) Explain how this reflex helps survival.

(a) A: sensory neurone, B: relay neurone, C: motor neurone.

(b) The small number of neurones in the reflex arc makes the response very fast, so you will quickly move your hand away from the flame. This helps survival because it reduces the risk of being burnt.

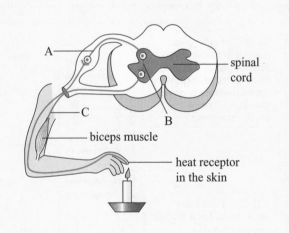

A — spinal cord

C

B

biceps muscle

heat receptor in the skin

The knee-jerk reflex arc contains only two neurones, but most contain at least three neurones.

Now try this

target G-D

1. Describe how you could test the sensitivity of different parts of the skin to touch.
   (2 marks)

target F-C

2. Explain why some responses that protect us from harm are controlled by reflex arcs.
   (2 marks)

target F-C

3. An electrical impulse cannot cross a synapse. Explain how a sensory neurone passes an impulse to a relay neurone. **(3 marks)**

Hormones

Chemical messengers

Hormones are 'chemical messengers'. They are produced by endocrine glands and released into the blood. They travel around the body in the blood until they reach their target organs. The hormone then causes the target organ to respond, e.g. by releasing another chemical.

Different hormones have different target organs and cause different responses.

Nerves and hormones both help us to respond to changes in the environment and in our bodies. Remember: nerve impulses are electrical signals in neurones, hormones are chemicals carried in the blood.

Worked example

Insulin is a hormone. Name the endocrine gland where insulin is made and its target organs, and explain how insulin reaches the target organs.

Insulin is made in the pancreas. Its target organs are muscles and liver cells. It travels from the pancreas to muscles and the liver in the blood.

Insulin

Insulin is the hormone that helps to regulate the concentration of glucose in the blood.

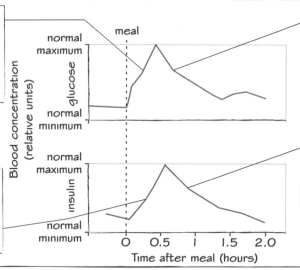

(1) Blood glucose concentration rises after a meal when sugars from digested carbohydrates enter the blood from the small intestine.

(2) The pancreas responds to a higher blood glucose concentration by releasing insulin into the blood.

(3) The insulin travels in the blood to muscle cells and liver cells. It causes these cells to take glucose out of the blood. This glucose is converted to glycogen and stored.

(4) As blood glucose concentration falls, the pancreas releases less insulin. So the amount of insulin in the blood falls.

Now try this

1. Choose the correct words to complete these sentences.

   (a) A hormone is an *electrical impulse/ chemical message*. **(1 mark)**

   (b) A hormone travels in *nerves/the blood* to its *endocrine gland/target organ*. **(2 marks)**

2. Describe the effect of the hormone insulin on the body. **(2 marks)**

3. Look at the graph of blood insulin concentration.

   (a) Explain why blood insulin concentration increases soon after eating a meal. **(2 marks)**

   (b) Explain why blood insulin concentration falls about 1.5 hours after a meal. **(2 marks)**

Diabetes

A person who cannot control their blood glucose concentration properly has a condition known as diabetes. There are two main types of diabetes.

Type 1 diabetes

People with Type 1 diabetes do not produce any insulin in their pancreas and so have to inject insulin into subcutaneous fat (the fat just below the skin). They have to work out the right amount of insulin to inject so that blood glucose concentration is kept within safe limits.

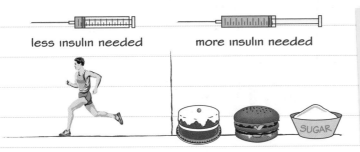

less insulin needed   more insulin needed

Glucose is used by cells during exercise, so less insulin is needed then. Glucose is taken into the blood from digested sugars. The more sugar there is in a meal, the more glucose enters the blood and the more insulin is needed.

Type 2 diabetes

People with Type 2 diabetes make insulin, but their liver and muscle cells have become resistant to it (they don't respond to it properly). Most people with Type 2 diabetes control their blood glucose concentration by:

- eating foods that contain less sugar
- exercising.

BMI and Type 2 diabetes

Body mass index (BMI) is calculated using this equation:

$$BMI = \frac{\text{weight in kilograms}}{(\text{height in metres})^2}$$

People who have a BMI over 30 are said to be obese. Obesity is linked with many health problems, including Type 2 diabetes.

Worked example

Use the graph to help you describe the correlation between obesity and Type 2 diabetes.

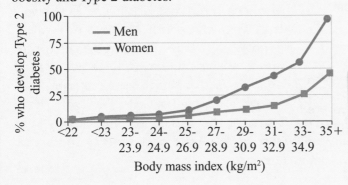

The higher your BMI, the higher your chance of developing Type 2 diabetes. This is true for both men and women, although the risk for women is higher.

A correlation is when two quantities increase (or decrease) together. A correlation shows that the two things may be related, but it does not prove that one change causes the other.

Now try this

target **G-D**

1. Describe the cause of Type 1 diabetes. **(1 mark)**

2. Tom is 1.8 m tall and weighs 100 kg. Calculate his BMI and say whether he is obese. **(3 marks)**

target **E-C**

3. Explain why exercising is recommended for people with diabetes. **(2 marks)**

Plant hormones

Tropism

A tropism is a plant's response to a stimulus (a change in the environment) by growing. A positive tropism is when the plant grows *towards* the stimulus.

- Plant shoots show positive phototropism because they grow towards light.
- Plant roots show positive gravitropism because they grow downwards – towards the pull of gravity. (Gravitropism is also called geotropism.)

Plant hormones

Plant hormones or plant growth substances are chemicals that cause changes in plants.

- Auxins are plant hormones that make cells grow longer.
- Gibberellins can make plant shoots grow longer. They also control when seeds germinate.

Auxins and tropisms

Auxins cause phototropism in shoots because they are affected by light.

In a shoot, where light is coming from one side:

| The light causes auxins to move to the shaded part of a shoot. | There are more auxins on the shaded side of a shoot. | So the cells on the shaded side grow longer than those on the lit side. | The tip of the shoot will end up growing towards the light. |

Worked example

The diagram shows the results of an experiment growing shoots in light from one direction. Explain what is happening to the auxins in each shoot.

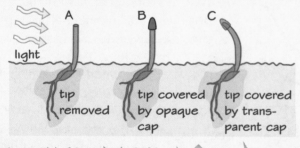

A shows that when the shoot tip is removed, the shoot doesn't grow, so that is where the auxins are made. B shows that when the shoot tip gets no light, it grows but doesn't bend because the auxins are not affected. C shows that as long as the shoot tip gets light, the shoot will grow towards the light. This is because the auxins are affected by light and move to the dark side of the shoot.

Now try this

 target G–D

1. (a) Describe positive phototropism in a shoot. **(2 marks)**

   (b) State whether gravitropism in a root is positive or negative. Explain your answer. **(2 marks)**

 target G–D

2. Name two types of plant growth substances. **(2 marks)**

3. Explain how auxin helps a shoot to grow towards light shining from one side. **(3 marks)**

Biology extended writing 3

Worked example

Question 1

The human body needs to keep at a fairly constant temperature of 37 °C in order to stay healthy. Keeping the body at this temperature is one of the roles of the hypothalamus. The hypothalamus brings about changes in the skin to help maintain body temperature.

Explain how these changes in the skin help the body to maintain its temperature. **(6 marks)**

Sample answer 1

If we get too hot, then we start to sweat. Sweat is made in glands in the skin. The hypothalamus sends messages to make this happen. Also, if we get too cold, the hairs on our skin stand on end.

This is a basic answer. It gives a basic description of two of the processes that control the temperature of the body. One improvement would be to mention more of the processes that happen, such as the changes in blood flow in the skin. The other problem is that the question said 'Explain...' but this answer does not explain how these processes help to maintain body temperature.

Sample answer 2

Sweating is an important way that the body controls its temperature. If we get hot, then sweat glands start to produce sweat. When sweat evaporates from the skin, it removes heat energy from the skin, which cools us down. Sweating stops if we are cool enough. The blood vessels in the skin also help to keep us cool. If we are hot, more blood flows near the surface of the skin. If we are cold, blood vessels change to keep the blood further below the skin surface.

This is a good answer. It says what happens in each process if the body is too hot and if it is too cold. This sort of comparison is a useful one to make. There is a good explanation of how sweating helps to maintain the body's temperature. The description of blood flow is also good — but the answer could be improved by explaining how this helps either keep heat in the body or helps to cool the body down. Further improvements could come from explaining the role of the hairs in the skin. Lastly, it would be good to use some more scientific words — here, the best one to use would be 'thermoregulation'.

Now try this

1. Compare the ways in which nerves and hormones carry messages around the body. **(6 marks)**

When answering this question there are lots of different ways to organise your answer. You could draw up a table. Or you could just write a few sentences on the way that nerves carry messages and the way that hormones carry messages. But you need to make sure that you compare the two systems and you must use full sentences and include all the relevant information.

21

Effects of drugs

Drugs

A drug is a chemical that affects the central nervous system. So a drug can change your psychological behaviour, which is the way you think or feel. For example, narcotics are drugs that make you feel sleepy.

Some drugs cause addiction. This means that the person becomes dependent on taking the drug and feels they cannot function properly without it.

Different types of drugs

 Painkillers
Example: morphine

Effect: block nerve impulses from pain receptors so you don't feel as much pain

 Hallucinogens
Example: LSD

Effect: change the way you experience a sense, e.g. colours may seem much brighter – can make it difficult to distinguish between what is or isn't real

 Depressants
Example: alcohol

Effect: increase reaction time – so you respond more slowly

 Stimulants
Example: caffeine

Effect: reduce reaction time by speeding up how fast synapses work – so you respond more quickly

Watch out! It is easy to be confused by reaction time. The faster you react to something, the shorter the reaction time.

Worked example

You can measure reaction time by catching a dropped ruler or using a test on the internet. Describe how you would test to see if caffeine in cola affected reaction time. Explain your answer.

To see if caffeine affects reaction time, you could compare reaction times with the same test measured after drinking normal cola, caffeine-free cola or water.

Comparing the results for normal and caffeine-free cola would show if caffeine has an effect. Comparing the results of water and caffeine-free cola would show if anything else in cola has an effect.

If you were asked to plan the experiment you would need to consider:

- the controlled variable (caffeine in the colas, and other chemicals in cola compared with water) and the measured variable (time taken to respond)
- controlling all other variables (e.g. time between drinking and carrying out the reaction test or the brand of cola)
- taking repeat measurements so you can calculate a mean value to average out random variation.

Now try this

target G-F

1. (a) Give an example of a depressant. **(1 mark)**
   (b) Describe the effect of a hallucinogen on the body. **(1 mark)**

target F-D

2. Morphine is a strong painkiller that is also a narcotic. Describe two effects that morphine has on the body. **(2 marks)**

target E-C

3. (a) Describe the effect you would expect caffeine to have on reaction time. **(1 mark)**
   (b) Explain your answer to part (a). **(2 marks)**

The damage caused by smoking

Tobacco smoke contains many chemicals that harm the body.

Nicotine is an addictive drug in tobacco smoke. It makes it difficult for people to give up smoking.

Carbon monoxide is a gas in tobacco smoke that can get into the blood from the lungs. Carbon monoxide in the blood reduces how much oxygen the red blood cells can carry.

Some of the chemicals in tar in tobacco smoke are carcinogens – they cause cancers. Smokers are more likely than non-smokers to get cancer of the mouth, throat and lungs.

Worked example

The table shows how many American men out of 1000 will die within 10 years from the age of 40 from several different causes. Use the table to discuss any correlation between smoking and these causes of death.

	Deaths per 1000 men		
	Heart disease	Lung cancer	Accidents
Non-smoker	1	1	5
Smoker	7	4	5

The data show that in every 1000 men who smoke:
- 6 more are likely to die of heart disease within 10 years than men who don't smoke.
- 3 more are likely to die of lung cancer within 10 years than men who don't smoke.
- the same number of non-smokers are likely to die from accidents within 10 years as men who don't smoke.

This suggests that smoking is correlated with an increased risk of heart disease and of lung cancer, but not an increased risk of a fatal accident.

Two factors show a correlation when they change in a similar way, e.g. as one goes up the other goes up.

If you were asked to evaluate these data, you would want to know how many people were in the survey. Generally, the more people you compare, the more reliable any conclusions will be.

Now try this

1. (a) State which chemical in tobacco smoke can cause cancers. **(1 mark)**
   (b) State which chemical in tobacco smoke reduces the amount of oxygen in the blood. **(1 mark)**

(a) Name the chemical in tobacco smoke that makes it difficult to give up smoking. **(1 mark)**
(b) Explain why the chemical you named in (a) has this effect. **(2 marks)**

2. Many smokers know that smoking can harm them but find it difficult to stop smoking.

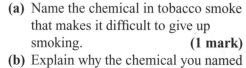

3. Explain why smokers are more likely to die of lung cancer than non-smokers. **(2 marks)**

The effects of alcohol

Drinking a lot of alcohol can harm the body.

Short-term harm

Short-term harm is caused by drinking a lot of alcohol at one time.

This can produce blurred vision and slow down reactions.

It can also make you less likely to think about what you are doing, so you may take more risks.

Long-term harm

Long-term harm is caused by drinking a lot of alcohol many times.

This can damage the brain and cause liver cirrhosis (liver damage).

Worked example

The graph shows results from a study of the risk of having an accident with different amounts of alcohol in the blood. Other studies show similar results.

(a) Draw a conclusion from the results shown in the graph.
(b) Explain your conclusion.
(c) Evaluate this evidence for the risks of alcohol.

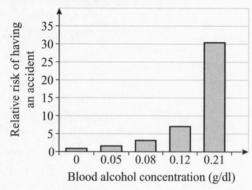

(a) Conclusion: As the concentration of alcohol increases in the blood, the risk of being involved in an accident also increases.

(b) Explanation: Alcohol is a depressant. This means it slows your reactions, so you take longer to make a decision.

(c) Evaluation: The evidence in the graph is reliable because other studies like this show the same pattern of results.

> Your conclusion must describe the full pattern of results in the graph. This includes using the word 'increase'. To say 'going up' may not be accurate enough.

> The question gives you the information for this answer. If many studies show the same result, the conclusion will be more reliable.

Now try this

target G-F

1. (a) Give one example of short-term harm caused to the body by too much alcohol. **(1 mark)**
   (b) Give one example of long-term harm caused to the body by too much alcohol. **(1 mark)**

target D-C

2. (a) Alcohol slows down responses. State what type of drug alcohol is. **(1 mark)**
   (b) Explain why it is illegal to drive with too much alcohol in your blood. **(2 marks)**

Ethics and transplants

Some diseases can be cured by transplanting a healthy organ from a person who has just died into a patient whose organ is damaged. There are never enough healthy organs available for all who need transplants, and many patients will die while waiting for an organ.

Ethical decisions

Ethical decisions are about what you think is right or wrong, or what is fair or unfair. Different people may make a different choice, depending on their point of view.

Obese patients

Some people think it is wrong that a clinically obese patient gets a heart transplant instead of a patient who is not as heavy, because an obese patient may not survive the operation as well as a lighter patient.

Other people think it is right that everyone is treated equally, because an obese patient may not be able to control their weight.

Donor cards

Some countries think it is right that people have to say if they *don't want* their organs to be used for transplants after they die. This policy can increase the number of organs available for transplant.

Other countries think it is right that people have to say if they *do want* their organs to be used for transplants after they die. This is because the relatives of the dead person may object.

Worked example

A hospital decides not to give liver transplants to patients with damaged livers until they have not drunk alcohol for 6 months.

(a) Suggest why the hospital made this decision.

(b) Explain why some people might think that this decision is unfair to alcoholics.

(a) A lot of alcohol damages the liver, and a person who has had a transplant will probably live longer if they don't drink much alcohol afterwards.

(b) An alcoholic finds it difficult to give up drinking alcohol. If their liver is badly damaged, they might die before they are able to control their drinking.

EXAM ALERT!

The answer should include the point of view of the hospital, and the point of view of an alcoholic patient.

Remember that the hospital may have to choose between patients because there may not be enough organs for all who need them.

Students have struggled with exam questions similar to this - **be prepared!**

Now try this

1. Describe what is meant by an ethical decision. **(1 mark)**

2. State one argument for asking people to say that they don't want their organs used for transplant after they die. **(1 mark)**

3. Explain why the decision by a hospital about which patients should get a liver transplant may be an ethical one. **(2 marks)**

Pathogens and infection

Spreading infection

Pathogens are spread in different ways. Some are spread by animals, which are called vectors. For example, *Anopheles* mosquitoes bite people to suck their blood. These mosquitoes are vectors for the malaria protozoan. While the mosquito is sucking blood, the pathogen leaves the mosquito and enters the human blood system.

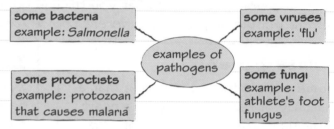

An infectious disease is one that can be passed from one person to another. A pathogen is an organism that causes an infectious disease.

some bacteria
example: *Salmonella*

examples of pathogens

some viruses
example: 'flu'

some protoctists
example: protozoan that causes malaria

some fungi
example: athlete's foot fungus

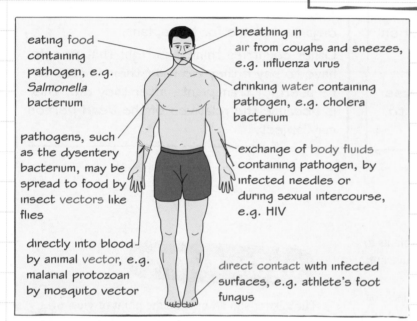

eating food containing pathogen, e.g. *Salmonella* bacterium

pathogens, such as the dysentery bacterium, may be spread to food by insect vectors like flies

directly into blood by animal vector, e.g. malarial protozoan by mosquito vector

breathing in air from coughs and sneezes, e.g. influenza virus

drinking water containing pathogen, e.g. cholera bacterium

exchange of body fluids containing pathogen, by infected needles or during sexual intercourse, e.g. HIV

direct contact with infected surfaces, e.g. athlete's foot fungus

Watch out! Vectors are not pathogens. Vectors carry pathogens from one person to another. Vectors are one way that infectious diseases are spread.

Worked example

Give examples of infectious diseases that are spread in two different ways.

Salmonella is a bacterium that causes food poisoning and is spread in food. Malaria is a disease caused by a protozoan that is carried between people by *Anopheles* mosquitoes, which act as a vector.

Now try this

target G-E

target G-D

1. Name one group of organisms that includes pathogens. **(1 mark)**

2. Describe the difference between a pathogen and a vector. **(2 marks)**

3. Describe five different ways in which pathogens can be spread. For each way, give an example of a pathogen spread that way. **(5 marks)**

Antiseptics and antibiotics

The human body protects itself against infection using physical barriers and chemical defences.

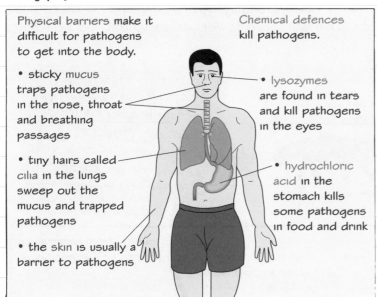

Physical barriers make it difficult for pathogens to get into the body.

- sticky mucus traps pathogens in the nose, throat and breathing passages

- tiny hairs called cilia in the lungs sweep out the mucus and trapped pathogens

- the skin is usually a barrier to pathogens

Chemical defences kill pathogens.

- lysozymes are found in tears and kill pathogens in the eyes

- hydrochloric acid in the stomach kills some pathogens in food and drink

More chemical defences

Many plants make chemicals that help to protect them from attack by bacterial pathogens. These chemicals are called antibacterials.

We use some of these antibacterials from plants to help protect us from infection. For example, menthol from mint helps to kill mouth bacteria when we use mint toothpaste to clean our teeth.

Remember: Antibiotics do not kill viruses, such as those that cause colds or flu.

Worked example

Complete the table with a definition for each word.

antibiotic	chemical taken as medicine that kills some kinds of pathogens after they have infected the body
antibacterial	chemical that kills bacteria or stops them growing
antifungal	chemical that kills fungi or stops them growing
antiseptic	chemical used to prevent infection by killing pathogens on surfaces before they can get into the body

Effect of antibiotics on bacteria

You can study the effect of antiseptics or antibiotics on the growth of microorganisms in a Petri dish. The larger the clear area around the chemical, the more effective it is at killing microorganisms.

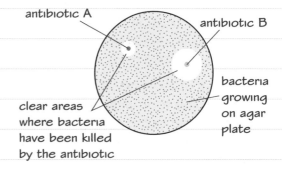

antibiotic A

antibiotic B

bacteria growing on agar plate

clear areas where bacteria have been killed by the antibiotic

Now try this

1. State one example of a chemical defence and one example of a physical barrier to infection. **(2 marks)**

2. (a) Identify one chemical that could be used to treat athlete's foot. **(1 mark)**

   (b) Explain your choice in part (a). **(1 mark)**

3. (a) Look at the agar plate above. Identify which antibiotic was the most effective at killing bacteria. **(1 mark)**

   (b) Explain your answer to part (a). **(1 mark)**

Interdependence and food webs

Chemical energy is transferred from organism to organism along a food chain or in a food web. All living organisms are interdependent (connected) due to their feeding relationships. These relationships are dynamic (always changing). For example, if there are more herbivores, they will eat more plants. This will leave fewer plants to eat, so some herbivores will then starve.

Energy transfers

energy is transferred along the food chain as chemical energy in the food that each animal eats

producer   primary consumer
(herbivore)   secondary consumer
(carnivore)

> Trophic levels are the feeding levels of a food chain: e.g. producer, primary consumer (herbivore), secondary consumer (carnivore).

Energy flow

light energy taken in during photosynthesis used to make new plant tissue

heat energy from respiration transferred to surroundings

chemical energy stored in biomass of food

heat energy from respiration transferred to surroundings

chemical energy stored in faeces and urine

> The biomass of an organism is the mass of its body tissue.

chemical energy stored as new plant tissue (biomass) which can be transferred to herbivores in their food

chemical energy stored as new animal tissue (biomass) which can be transferred to carnivores in their food

Pyramids of biomass

A pyramid of biomass is a diagram that shows the amount of biomass (usually as g/m²) at each trophic level of a food chain. The producer level is the bottom bar, and the other bars show the trophic levels in order.

The amount of biomass at each trophic level along the food chain gets smaller. This is because some energy at each level is transferred as heat energy to the environment.

Food chains are usually no more than 4 or 5 trophic levels long because there is not enough biomass in the top level to provide the energy needed by another trophic level.

The food chain for this pyramid is:
lettuce → caterpillar → thrush

thrush   12 g/m²

caterpillars   60 g/m²

lettuces   120 g/m²

EXAM ALERT!

If you are asked to draw a pyramid of biomass make sure that the sizes of the blocks representing each trophic level are in proportion to the amount of biomass given.

Students have struggled with this topic in recent exams – **be prepared!**   ResultsPlus

Parasites and mutualists

Most plants are producers and most animals are consumers. In other feeding relationships one organism depends on the presence of another living species.

Parasitism

A parasite feeds on another organism (the host) while they are living together. Taking food from the host usually harms it but doesn't kill it. A parasite may be a plant or an animal.

Parasite	Host	Description
flea (animal)	other animals, including humans	fleas feed by sucking the animal's blood after piercing its skin
head louse (animal)	humans	head lice feed by sucking blood after piercing the skin on the head
tapeworm (animal)	other animals, including humans	tapeworms live in the animal's intestine and absorb nutrients from the digested food in the intestine
mistletoe (plant)	trees, e.g. apple	mistletoe grows roots into the tree to absorb water and nutrients from the host

Mutualism

When two organisms live closely together in a way that helps them both, they are called mutualists.

Oxpeckers are African birds that eat insects which are parasites of large animals such as wild cattle. The oxpeckers benefit because they get food. The cattle benefit because their parasites are removed.

> Watch out! A parasite harms a host organism by taking food from it while they live together. If you just say that 'a parasite feeds on other organisms', you could also be talking about predators. Predators don't live attached to their prey.

Worked example

Cleaner fish are small fish that feed on dead skin and parasites of larger fish. Explain why this is a mutualist relationship.

The cleaner fish benefit by getting food. The larger fish benefit by getting rid of parasites that may harm them. So both organisms benefit from the relationship.

> In a mutualist relationship, you must show how *both* organisms benefit.

Now try this

1. Choose the correct meaning for the term parasite. **(1 mark)**
   (a) An organism that feeds on other organisms.
   (b) An organism that harms another organism by feeding on it while they are living together.
   (c) An organism that lives with another organism without harming it.

2. The human flea is a parasite of humans.
   (a) Describe how the flea gets its food. **(1 mark)**
   (b) Explain why this is a parasitic relationship. **(1 mark)**

3. Explain what is meant by a mutualist relationship. **(1 mark)**

Pollution

Global human population change

The global human population is increasing. This is because each year the number of babies born is greater than the number of people who die. As human population increases, pollution will increase unless we find ways to reduce the amount of pollutants we produce.

Worked example

The graph shows the best estimate of the number of people in the world since 1950, and three predictions of population size in 2050. Analyse and interpret the graph.

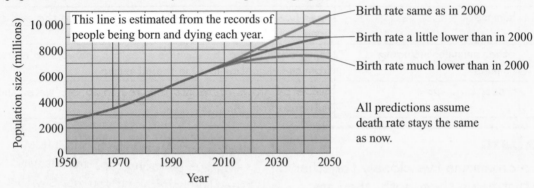

This line is estimated from the records of people being born and dying each year.

Birth rate same as in 2000

Birth rate a little lower than in 2000

Birth rate much lower than in 2000

All predictions assume death rate stays the same as now.

The graph shows that human population size has risen since 1950 from about 2500 million to nearly 7000 million now. The three different estimates of population size depend on differences in possible birth rates. The high and medium estimates show population size will continue to rise. The low estimate shows that it will level out at about 7500 million in 2030–2040 and then start to fall.

Pollution

Some human activities cause pollution. A pollutant is a substance that can damage the environment and the organisms that live in it. Pollutants include:

- sulfur dioxide gas released from factories and power stations, which pollutes the air
- phosphates and nitrates from sewage and fertiliser, which can pollute water.

Eutrophication

Fertilisers added to fields for crops may get into streams and rivers. This adds phosphates and nitrates to the water, which is called eutrophication.

Eutrophication causes water plants and algae to grow more quickly.	Plants and algae cover the water surface, and block light to deeper water.	Deeper plants cannot get light, so they die.	Bacteria decompose dying plants and take oxygen from the water.	There is not enough oxygen left in the water for fish, so they die.

Now try this

target **G-D**

1. Explain what a pollutant is.
     (1 mark)

target **E-C**

2. Explain why pollution may increase over the next 50 years. **(2 marks)**

target **E-C**

3. Explain how eutrophication might cause fish to die. **(4 marks)**

Pollution indicators

Some species are well adapted to living in polluted conditions. Other species can only live where there is no pollution. The presence or absence of these indicator species can show us whether or not there is pollution.

Indicators of air pollution	Indicators of water pollution
Some species of lichen can only grow where there is no pollution. Other species can grow where there is air pollution. So the species of lichen growing on trees can tell you if the air has been polluted.	Bloodworms and sludgeworms can live in water that contains little oxygen. So they are found in polluted water.
Blackspot is a fungus that infects roses. The fungus is damaged by sulfur dioxide in the air. So where there is air pollution, the roses are clear of the fungus.	Stonefly larvae (young stonefly) and freshwater shrimps can only live in water that contains a lot of oxygen. So they are indicators of unpolluted water.

Recycling

Recycling means to re-use materials. Materials that are commonly recycled include metals, paper and plastics.

EXAM ALERT!

Saying that recycling is 'better for the environment' is not enough. You have to link the recycling to saving energy and conserving resources. You are often asked to make links like this.

Students have struggled with exam questions similar to this - **be prepared!**

ResultsPlus

Worked example

Explain how recycling metals, paper and plastics can reduce the amount of landfill and conserve resources.

When metals such as steel and aluminium are recycled, less metal ore has to be extracted from the ground. For most metals, less energy is needed to recycle than produce these new metals, so this also saves resources.

When paper is recycled to make paper or cardboard, this means that trees do not have to be cut down to make new paper. It also takes less energy to recycle paper than make it new from trees.

Recycling plastics saves using oil to make new plastic.

Recycling any material also reduces the amount of waste that we incinerate or dump into landfill tips.

Now try this

 target G-D
1. For each of these organisms, state if its presence indicates that there is pollution or that there is no pollution:
   (a) stonefly larva　　**(1 mark)**
   (b) sludgeworm　　　**(1 mark)**
   (c) blackspot on roses.　**(1 mark)**

 target G-D
2. Explain how each of the species in question 1 acts as an indicator species.
   (3 marks)

target E-C
3. Describe two benefits to the environment for recycling materials.　**(2 marks)**

The carbon cycle

The carbon cycle can be represented by a diagram to show how the element carbon passes between the environment and living organisms. In the air, the carbon is part of carbon dioxide gas.

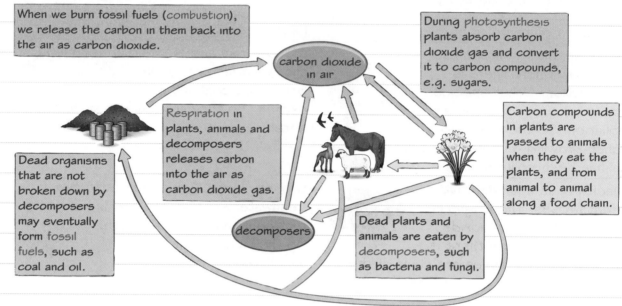

When we burn fossil fuels (combustion), we release the carbon in them back into the air as carbon dioxide.

During photosynthesis plants absorb carbon dioxide gas and convert it to carbon compounds, e.g. sugars.

Respiration in plants, animals and decomposers releases carbon into the air as carbon dioxide gas.

Dead organisms that are not broken down by decomposers may eventually form fossil fuels, such as coal and oil.

Carbon compounds in plants are passed to animals when they eat the plants, and from animal to animal along a food chain.

Dead plants and animals are eaten by decomposers, such as bacteria and fungi.

carbon dioxide in air

decomposers

Worked example

A large forest is cleared by burning. What effects will this have on the amount of carbon dioxide in the air (a) immediately, (b) over a longer period?

(a) Large amounts of carbon dioxide will be released into the air by the burning (combustion) of the trees.

(b) Less carbon dioxide will be removed from the air than before because the trees would have used some for photosynthesis. So the amount of carbon dioxide in the air is likely to remain high.

EXAM ALERT!

In questions about the carbon cycle, you will be expected to make links between photosynthesis, respiration and combustion, and the amount of carbon dioxide in the air.

Students have struggled with exam questions similar to this - **be prepared!**

ResultsPlus

Now try this

target G-E

1. State the substance in the air that contains carbon atoms. **(1 mark)**

2. Match each process to what it does in the carbon cycle. **(2 marks)**

Process	Role in the carbon cycle
combustion	releases carbon from compounds in living organisms as carbon dioxide gas into the air
photosynthesis	releases carbon from compounds in fossil fuels as carbon dioxide gas into the air
respiration	changes carbon dioxide gas into carbon compounds in living organisms

target E-C

3. Describe what decomposers do in the carbon cycle. **(2 marks)**

Biology extended writing 4

Worked example

Question 1

Drinks such as beer, wine and vodka contain alcohol. Although alcohol is a depressant, people often enjoy the social effects of drinking. However, drinking too much alcohol is bad for your health.

Describe the short-term and the long-term effects of alcohol abuse. **(6 marks)**

Sample answer 1

People who drink alcohol may get drunk. This often means that they appear to be more friendly. This is a short-term effect and wears off, leaving people with a hangover. Another serious short-term effect is that people might drive and crash their car. People who drink over a long period might suffer from problems with their liver, or become addicted to alcohol. These are long-term effects.

This is a good answer. It is clear from the answer which are short-term and which are long-term effects. The answer mentions a good number of both effects and there is a brief description. Although it is good, the answer would be better if it included a little more scientific explanation, such as explaining that alcohol slows down reaction times.

Sample answer 2

Alcohol is a drug and it affects the way in which the brain works. It is a depressant so, although it makes people feel more relaxed, it slows down reaction times. This is very dangerous if people drink and drive. Vision can also be affected by the alcohol, which can also affect driving. These effects are short term, as they wear off. However, if you often drink too much, your liver may be damaged by cirrhosis. Like most drugs, alcohol is addictive and people may get dependent on it. This could affect the way in which you get on with your family and friends.

This is an excellent answer. Notice that it has introduced some more scientific words into the answer. The most obvious are words like 'cirrhosis', but note also the way in which the description of alcohol as a drug appears both in short-term and long-term effects. Also, the answer considers the effects on alcohol on biological systems – the brain, the eyes and the liver. The long-term effect of alcohol on the brain could also be added.

Now try this

1. Describe ways in which smoking cigarettes is bad for human health. **(6 marks)**

Biology extended writing 5

Worked example

Question 1

Artificial fertilisers are often used to improve the yield of different crops. They work by providing the nitrogen needed for plants to grow.

Explain how using too much fertiliser on crops can cause problems in the environment.   **(6 marks)**

Sample answer 1

If farmers use too much fertiliser, it gets into the water and can run off into rivers and lakes. The fertiliser is a pollutant and it can cause fish and plants living in the river to die. This is called eutrophication. Once this happens the water cannot support any living creatures.

Although this answer uses a very important word ('eutrophication'), it is still a basic answer. This is mostly because the answer doesn't explain what eutrophication actually means! This would be an obvious improvement for the answer – to describe what happens in eutrophication.

The answer has told us that eutrophication kills organisms, but it would be better if it described why this happened.

Sample answer 2

Rain carries the fertiliser into rivers and lakes. The adding of nutrients such as nitrates to the water is called eutrophication. The fertiliser makes algae grow on the surface of the water. This blocks out sunlight, so that other water plants cannot photosynthesise. The plants die and microorganisms in the water start to break them down. The microorganisms respire and this means that they remove oxygen from the water. This lack of oxygen means that fish and other organisms in the river also die.

This is an excellent answer. It covers all the major points and it puts the events into a logical sequence. The answer also uses a range of biological language and terms that show a very good understanding of the subject.

Now try this

1. Explain how carbon dioxide is added to and removed from the air in the carbon cycle.   **(6 marks)**

Your answer should name the processes in the cycle and say how and why each one changes the amount of carbon dioxide in the air.

The early atmosphere

The Earth's first atmosphere

The Earth's first atmosphere was formed by gases produced from volcanoes.

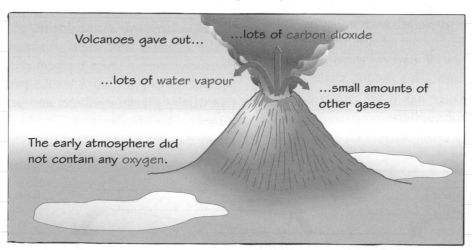

Volcanoes gave out...

...lots of carbon dioxide

...lots of water vapour

...small amounts of other gases

The early atmosphere did not contain any oxygen.

The Earth was very hot to start with, and there were no oceans. As the Earth cooled down the water vapour in the atmosphere condensed to form liquid water. This liquid water became the oceans.

Worked example

Explain why scientists cannot be certain about the composition of the early atmosphere.

There were no humans around to measure the atmosphere, so they have to use clues. There are different sources of information, but not all the evidence leads to the same conclusion. This means that it is difficult to know exactly what the early atmosphere was like and how it has changed.

The evidence includes:

- the gases produced by volcanoes today, which tell us what gases would have been produced by volcanoes in the past
- the atmospheres of other planets and moons in the solar system, where the atmosphere has not been changed by living things
- iron compounds found in very old rocks that could only form if there was no oxygen.

You don't need to remember these different sources of information. You DO need to remember that there ARE different sources of information, some of which tell us different things.

Now try this

target
G-D

1. (a) Name the two gases present in the largest amounts in the Earth's early atmosphere. **(2 marks)**
    (b) State where scientists think these gases came from. **(1 mark)**

2. Describe how the Earth's oceans formed. **(2 marks)**

A changing atmosphere

Early Earth

The atmosphere of the early Earth was mainly carbon dioxide, with little or no oxygen. Today the atmosphere has much less than 1% carbon dioxide and has 21% oxygen. This means that:

- carbon dioxide has been removed from the atmosphere
- oxygen has been added to the atmosphere.

Adding oxygen

The first organisms that evolved on Earth did not use or release oxygen. About a billion years ago some forms of life evolved in the oceans that used photosynthesis. Photosynthesis uses carbon dioxide and produces oxygen as a waste product. Eventually plants evolved and some of them adapted to life on land. Gradually, more and more oxygen was added to the atmosphere.

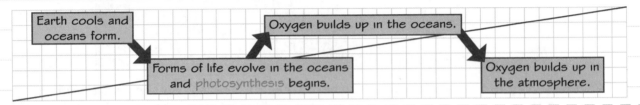

| Earth cools and oceans form. | → | Forms of life evolve in the oceans and photosynthesis begins. | → | Oxygen builds up in the oceans. | → | Oxygen builds up in the atmosphere. |

Removing carbon dioxide

| Carbon dioxide dissolved in the oceans. | → | Marine organisms used the dissolved carbon dioxide to make calcium carbonate for shells. | → | The shells of dead marine organisms fall to the sea bed and become part of the sediment. | → | Over millions of years the layers of sediment become squashed and form sedimentary rocks. |

Worked example

There is a lot of limestone in the Earth's crust.
Explain how the formation of limestone removes carbon dioxide from the Earth's atmosphere.

Some carbon dioxide in the atmosphere dissolves in the oceans. Some marine organisms use dissolved carbon dioxide to make calcium carbonate for their shells. When they die, these marine organisms sink to the sea bed and their shells eventually form limestone. The carbon locked up in the limestone originally came from the atmosphere.

You need to explain the link between limestone and carbon by saying that limestone is made from shells, which are mostly calcium carbonate.

In an exam you could present the answer to this kind of question as a flow chart.

Now try this

target **G–D**

1. State how the percentage of carbon dioxide changed from the Earth's early atmosphere to the amount in today's atmosphere. **(1 mark)**

2. (a) State the main substance in the shells of marine organisms. **(1 mark)**
   (b) Describe how the shells change into limestone. **(3 marks)**

target **D–C**

3. Explain why the amount of oxygen in the atmosphere only started to increase about 1 billion years ago. **(2 marks)**

The atmosphere today

The amounts of different gases in the atmosphere are shown in the pie chart and table. The atmosphere also contains water vapour, but this is not usually included because the amount changes depending on the weather.

The composition of the atmosphere

Gas	% in dry air
nitrogen	78
oxygen	21
argon	0.9
carbon dioxide	0.04
other gases	traces

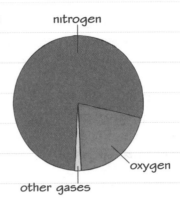

Changes in the atmosphere

The composition of the atmosphere today is not constant. It can be changed by human activities.

- Burning fossil fuels releases carbon dioxide into the atmosphere. Sulfur dioxide can also be released from burning coal.
- Farming affects the atmosphere, as cattle and rice fields release methane.
- Deforestation adds carbon dioxide to the atmosphere if the trees are burnt. There are also fewer trees to remove carbon dioxide from the atmosphere through photosynthesis.

Worked example

Explain one natural cause of changes in the atmosphere.

When volcanoes erupt they release a lot of sulfur dioxide into the atmosphere. They also release carbon dioxide.

Remember that sulfur dioxide is also added to the atmosphere when fossil fuels such as coal are burnt.

Now try this

target
G-D

1. Name the gas that is present in the largest amount in air. **(1 mark)**

2. (a) State two human activities that add carbon dioxide to the atmosphere. **(2 marks)**

   (b) Name one other gas that human activities add to the atmosphere. **(1 mark)**

3. What changes to the atmosphere can occur naturally? **(2 marks)**

There are two marks for this question, so you need to mention two different natural changes.

Rocks and their formation

Rocks make up the Earth's crust.

Igneous rocks

Igneous rocks:

- are formed when magma or lava solidifies
- are made of interlocking crystals, which makes them hard and resistant to erosion
- have small crystals if the liquid rock cooled quickly (e.g. basalt)
- have large crystals if the liquid rock cooled slowly (e.g. granite).

> Watch out! magma is liquid rock *beneath* the Earth's surface. Liquid rock is called lava when it is *on* the surface of the Earth.

> If the rock cools down *slowly*, the crystals have more time to grow bigger.

Magnified view of interlocking crystals

Sedimentary rocks

Sedimentary rocks:

- are formed when layers of sediment are compacted (squashed together) over a very long time by being buried under more layers
- erode (wear away) more easily than igneous and metamorphic rocks
- are made of rounded grains and may contain fossils (the remains or traces of living organisms)
- include chalk and limestone, which are natural forms of calcium carbonate.

Magnified view of grains in a sedimentary rock

Metamorphic rocks

Worked example

Explain how metamorphic rocks are formed, and give an example of a metamorphic rock.

Metamorphic rocks are formed from existing rocks by the action of heat (from being buried or from nearby magma) and/ or pressure (from being buried), which causes new interlocking crystals to grow. Marble is a metamorphic rock which is formed from chalk or limestone.

> Marble is also a natural form of calcium carbonate.

EXAM ALERT!

You need to revise how different rocks are formed. For example, to answer this question fully you would need to explain that metamorphic rocks are formed by heat and pressure.

Students have struggled with exam questions similar to this - **be prepared!**   ResultsPlus

Now try this

target
G-D

1. Write down the names of two:
   (a) sedimentary rocks   **(2 marks)**
   (b) igneous rocks.   **(2 marks)**

2. Explain why granite has bigger crystals than basalt.   **(2 marks)**

target
D-C

3. Suggest why sedimentary rocks erode more easily than other types of rock.
      (1 mark)

Limestone and its uses

Using limestone

Limestone is used for making buildings, and as the base for roads and railways. Limestone is mostly made of calcium carbonate, and this substance is an important raw material used to make glass, cement and concrete.

Limestone is heated when making cement and glass. The heat decomposes (breaks down) the calcium carbonate in it to form calcium oxide and carbon dioxide. This process is called thermal decomposition.

$$\text{calcium carbonate} \rightarrow \text{calcium oxide} + \text{carbon dioxide}$$

Worked example

What is the most important use of limestone?

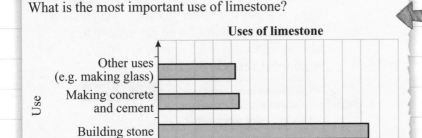

Uses of limestone

Building stone

EXAM ALERT!

Some questions in the exam may ask you to read data from a bar chart or graph. Make sure that you use only the relevant data from the bar chart and don't just write down everything.

Students have struggled with exam questions similar to this - **be prepared!**   Results**Plus**

Quarrying – good or bad?

We need to quarry a lot of limestone, but quarrying has economic, environmental and social effects. We need to balance the effects with the demand.

Advantages	Disadvantages
✓ Limestone is an important raw material.	✗ Quarries produce dust and noise.
✓ Quarries provide jobs in the countryside.	✗ Quarries spoil the scenery (although they are usually landscaped after quarrying has finished and can become wildlife reserves or recreation areas).
✓ Some limestone is exported to other countries, which helps the UK economy.	
✓ Jobs in quarries also help local economies, because the workers spend their money in local shops and businesses.	✗ Lorries taking the limestone away cause extra traffic, noise and pollution.

Now try this

target G-D

1. State three things that are made using limestone. **(3 marks)**

2. Explain what is meant by 'thermal decomposition'. **(2 marks)**

target D-C

3. A new limestone quarry is being created near a village.
   (a) State one economic advantage to people in the local area. **(1 mark)**
   (b) State one environmental disadvantage to the local area. **(1 mark)**

Compounds and formulae

Elements and molecules

An element is a substance that cannot be split into simpler substances. An atom is the smallest part of an element that can take part in chemical reactions. A molecule is two or more atoms chemically joined together.

A compound is a substance that consists of atoms of different elements joined together. A mixture contains different elements or compounds, but they are not chemically joined.

During a chemical reaction the atoms in the reactants are rearranged to make different products.

Chemical symbols

Each element has its own chemical symbol.

Chemical formulae

The formula of a compound shows the symbols of the elements it contains and the numbers of their atoms in the molecules. The atoms of some elements form molecules, so these elements have a formula as well.

O_2

Oxygen molecules are made up of two atoms of oxygen joined together.

The symbol for an element has one or two letters. If it has two letters, the first letter is always a capital letter and the second one a lower case letter. Some of the symbols are obvious (such as H for hydrogen). Some of the symbols are based on the names of elements in other languages and don't make much sense. You just have to learn them!

Worked example

Carbon dioxide is one atom of carbon (symbol C) chemically joined to two atoms of oxygen (O). Write the formula for carbon dioxide, and draw a carbon dioxide molecule.

CO_2

The small 2 after the O shows that there are two atoms of oxygen in every molecule of carbon dioxide.

Remember that the little number comes after the symbol for the element it refers to. So in water (H_2O) the 2 means there are two hydrogen atoms for every oxygen atom.

Now try this

 target G-D

1. The formula for calcium carbonate is $CaCO_3$. Name the three elements in calcium carbonate. **(3 marks)**

2. Draw diagrams like the ones above to show the molecules represented by these formulae. Label the atoms with their symbols. **(2 marks)**
   (a) H_2 (b) SO_2

3. For each of the formulae in question 2, say whether it represents an element or a compound. **(2 marks)**

Chemical reactions

In a chemical reaction atoms are rearranged to form different substances. The atoms are not created or destroyed. There are the same number of each type of atom present before and after the reaction – they are just joined up in different combinations. As no atoms have been created or destroyed, the total mass of all the atoms involved stays the same.

Word equations

Chemical reactions can be represented using word equations. The products of a reaction have different properties to the reactants.

zinc carbonate → zinc oxide + carbon dioxide

The reactants are on the left-hand side.

The products are on the right-hand side.

Thermal decomposition

Metal carbonates decompose when they are heated to form an oxide and carbon dioxide. Some carbonates decompose more easily than others (decomposition happens at a lower temperature).

copper carbonate — easiest to decompose

zinc carbonate

calcium carbonate — hardest to decompose

Worked example

A student uses this apparatus to investigate the thermal decomposition of copper carbonate, calcium carbonate and zinc carbonate. Explain which carbonate will take the shortest time to make the limewater turn milky.

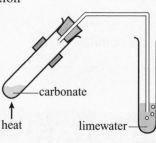

The copper carbonate is the easiest to decompose so it will take the shortest time to produce enough carbon dioxide to make the limewater turn milky.

Precipitation reactions

A precipitation reaction happens when two soluble substances react together to form a product that is insoluble. The insoluble product is the precipitate.

lead nitrate + potassium iodide → potassium nitrate + lead iodide
(soluble)   (soluble)   (soluble)   (insoluble – forms a precipitate)

You can use a precipitation reaction in a sealed container to demonstrate that the total mass before and after a reaction does not change.

Now try this

1. (a) Write a word equation for the thermal decomposition of copper carbonate. **(2 marks)**
   (b) State the reactant or reactants in this reaction. **(1 mark)**

2. A student mixes 1 g of silver nitrate solution with 2 g of potassium bromide solution. State the total mass of the mixture after a precipitation reaction occurs. **(1 mark)**

Reactions of calcium compounds

Limestone and marble are made of calcium carbonate.

Limewater is used to test for carbon dioxide. If carbon dioxide is bubbled through limewater it forms insoluble calcium carbonate.
This turns the limewater cloudy.

add CO_2

When calcium carbonate is heated it undergoes thermal decomposition to form calcium oxide and carbon dioxide.

calcium carbonate

heat

→ and CO_2

calcium hydroxide

calcium oxide

add water

When water is added to calcium oxide a lot of heat is released. The mixture fizzes, steam is given off and the calcium oxide crumbles to a white powder of calcium hydroxide. If more water is added to the reactants, the calcium hydroxide dissolves to form a solution called limewater.

EXAM ALERT!

Sometimes an exam question may ask you to describe what you see when a reaction happens. Make sure you only write about what you can *see*.

Students have struggled with this topic in recent exams - **be prepared!**   ResultsPlus

Word equations

calcium carbonate → calcium oxide + carbon dioxide

calcium oxide + water → calcium hydroxide

calcium hydroxide + carbon dioxide → calcium carbonate

Using calcium compounds

Calcium carbonate, calcium oxide and calcium hydroxide can all be used to neutralise acidic compounds. (There is more about neutralisation on page 45.)

Some soils are acidic. Farmers use calcium compounds to neutralise the acidity so their crops will grow better.

This paragraph explains how calcium carbonate is used to clean up the gases.
You will learn more about acid rain on page 58.

Worked example

Explain why the gases emitted by coal-fired power stations need to be cleaned up, and how calcium carbonate can be used to do this.

The waste gases from coal-fired power stations contain sulfur dioxide and nitrogen oxides, which are acidic gases. These gases cause acid rain if they get into the atmosphere.

Wet, powdered calcium carbonate is sprayed into the waste gases to neutralise them.

Now try this

target
G-F

target
G-D

1. Describe what you see when carbon dioxide is bubbled through limewater. **(1 mark)**

2. Explain why calcium oxide and calcium hydroxide are useful to farmers. **(2 marks)**

3. Describe what you would see when a few drops of water are added to a lump of calcium oxide. **(3 marks)**

Chemistry extended writing 1

To answer an extended writing question successfully you need to:
- ✓ use your scientific knowledge to answer the question
- ✓ organise your answer so that it is logical and well ordered
- ✓ use full sentences in your writing and make sure that your spelling, punctuation and grammar are correct.

Worked example

Question 1

A quarry company has applied to the local council for permission to dig a new quarry. The quarry will be in a scenic area that attracts walkers and bird watchers.

Discuss the possible effects on the local community that the council should consider when deciding whether or not to give permission. You should include social, economic and environmental impacts. **(6 marks)**

Sample answer 1

The quarry will provide jobs. Limestone is an important rock and a lot is exported. There will be more traffic on the roads. House prices will go down and wildlife may be affected and the scenery will be spoiled.

This is a basic answer. The question asked about the effects on the local community, so the comment about limestone being exported does not gain any credit because it is not relevant to the question. There are several disadvantages given, but the answer is not very well organised.

Sample answer 2

Social effects would be that lorries and dust would disturb local people. When the quarry is finished it might be turned into a park or nature reserve.

Economic effects would be to provide some jobs for local people. If more local people have jobs, they will spend more money in local shops and other businesses, so the local economy as a whole could benefit. But if the quarry stops some tourists from coming, this could have a bad effect on some businesses such as hotels and cafes.

Environmental effects would be destroying habitats for birds when the quarry is dug. The quarrying will produce dust and noise which might scare animals.

This is an excellent answer because it gives several advantages and disadvantages. The answer is well organised, with the different types of factor grouped together. There are not many scientific words used here, but the answer correctly uses words such as 'local economy'.

Now try this

1. When the Earth was formed its atmosphere was mostly carbon dioxide.

   Explain how the amount of carbon dioxide in the atmosphere has changed from the early atmosphere up to the present day. **(6 marks)**

Indigestion

Stomach acid

Our stomachs produce hydrochloric acid.
The acid is used to:

Stomach acid is always hydrochloric acid.

- kill bacteria in our food

- help digestion, as some of the enzymes that break down our food into simpler substances only work in acidic conditions.

Sometimes our stomachs produce too much acid. This causes pain that we call indigestion.

Neutralisation

Indigestion remedies contain antacids that neutralise excess stomach acid. Neutral liquids are neither acid nor alkaline.

Antacids contain substances called bases. Bases react with acids and neutralise them. Some bases are soluble. A base dissolved in water is called an alkali.

acid + base → salt + water

Worked example

An antacid contains magnesium hydroxide. Write the word equation for the reaction between hydrochloric acid and magnesium hydroxide.

hydrochloric acid + magnesium hydroxide → magnesium chloride + water

It helps if you remember the general equation for the reactions between acids and bases. Just write out the acid and base that you are given, then work out the name of the salt.

Don't forget to include the water!

Testing indigestion remedies

Neutral liquids have a pH of 7. Acids have a pH less than 7. When an indigestion remedy is added to an acid, it will neutralise some of the acid and the pH will increase.

To make this investigation a fair test, you must use the same volume of acid each time at the same concentration, and use one dose of each indigestion remedy. The remedy that produces the highest pH at the end has neutralised the most acid.

Now try this

target
G-D

1. State two reasons why our stomachs produce hydrochloric acid. **(2 marks)**

2. State what causes indigestion. **(1 mark)**

3. Complete the general word equation:
   acid + base → _____ + _____
   (2 marks)

4. State the pH of water. **(1 mark)**

Neutralisation

Neutralising acids

There are three different types of compound that can be used to neutralise acids:

- metal oxides (such as copper oxide)
- metal hydroxides (such as sodium hydroxide)
- metal carbonates (such as copper carbonate).

Make sure that you know what scientific words like 'neutralise' mean and then use them correctly in the exam.

Word equations

You need to learn these general equations. You might have to apply them in your exam.

acid + metal oxide → salt + water

acid + metal hydroxide → salt + water

acid + metal carbonate → salt + water + carbon dioxide

Watch out! These are the *only* kinds of metal compounds that can be used to neutralise acids. And don't forget that carbonates produce carbon dioxide as well as salt and water.

Naming salts

A salt is a compound made from a metal and a non-metal. The non-metal part of the salt comes from the acid. The metal part of the salt comes from the base or alkali used to neutralise it.

- hydrochloric acid produces chloride salts
- nitric acid produces nitrate salts
- sulfuric acid produces sulfate salts

Worked example

Complete this word equation:

nitric acid + sodium hydroxide

→ sodium nitrate + water

The first part of the name of the base is a metal. This metal is the first part of the name of the salt formed in the reaction.

Hazard symbols

Acids are hazardous substances and can be dangerous if not used properly. Containers of acids have hazard symbols on them. These standard symbols warn people about the hazards. People can then look up the precautions they should take to stay safe when working with these substances.

These hazard symbols are used on containers of acid.

Caution (harmful or irritant) Precautions: wear goggles and avoid getting the substance on your skin. Do not sniff the substance, and wash your hands after use.

Corrosive Precautions: wear gloves and goggles. Work in a well-ventilated area.

Now try this

target G-D

target D-C

1. Name three types of metal compound that can be used to neutralise acids. **(3 mark)**

2. Explain why containers of acid have hazard symbols on them. **(3 marks)**

3. Write word equations for the reactions between:

   (a) magnesium oxide and sulfuric acid **(3 marks)**

   (b) hydrochloric acid and copper carbonate. **(3 marks)**

The importance of chlorine

Compounds can be decomposed (broken up) using electricity. This process is called electrolysis. Electrolysis only works with a direct current (d.c.) such as the current from batteries.

Electrolysis

The apparatus in the diagram can be used to decompose dilute hydrochloric acid. Hydrogen gas is produced at one electrode, and chlorine gas is produced at the other.

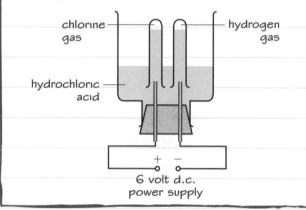

chlorine gas — hydrogen gas

hydrochloric acid

+ −
6 volt d.c. power supply

Using chlorine

Sea water contains a lot of dissolved sodium chloride. Chlorine gas can be obtained from sea water by electrolysis. Chlorine is used to make bleach, and to make plastics such as poly(chloroethene) (also called PVC).

You need to know the chemical symbols and formulae for the substances you learn about. The symbol for chlorine is Cl. This is always a capital 'C' with a small 'l'.

Chlorine gas is made of molecules with two chlorine atoms joined together. The formula for chlorine gas is Cl_2.

Dangers of chlorine

Chlorine is a toxic gas. This makes it useful as a disinfectant because it kills microorganisms. This also makes chlorine hazardous. Chlorine is very useful in industry, and millions of tonnes of it are produced every year. Accidental leaks of chlorine from factories or from tankers could harm or kill many people.

Worked example

Containers of chlorine are labelled with the 'toxic' hazard symbol.

Explain the precautions you should take if you are carrying out electrolysis of hydrochloric acid in the school laboratory.

Toxic

The laboratory must be well ventilated, by keeping the doors and some windows open. Take care not to sniff the gases produced.

These precautions are needed because the electrolysis of hydrochloric acid produces chlorine. Chlorine is a toxic gas, so it will harm you if you breathe it.

The question asks you to 'explain', so you must say why the precautions are needed.

Now try this

target
G-D

1. Name the two gases produced by the electrolysis of hydrochloric acid.
(2 marks)

2. State two uses of chlorine. **(2 marks)**

target
D-C

3. Explain why the laboratory must be well ventilated if you are carrying out electrolysis of sea water. **(3 marks)**

The electrolysis of water

Electrolysis

Water is a compound. The electrolysis of water produces hydrogen gas and oxygen gas.

Water molecules contain two atoms of hydrogen chemically joined to one atom of oxygen. The formula of water is H_2O. Electrolysis decomposes water into hydrogen (H_2) and oxygen (O_2).

Hydrogen

Hydrogen is a flammable gas. It can explode when it is mixed with air. Containers of hydrogen have the flammable hazard symbol on them.

Flammable

Remember that electrolysis only works with a direct current (d.c.). Alternating current (like the current from the mains supply) does not work.

Testing gases

The gases produced in reactions can be tested to find out what they are.

Gas	Hydrogen	Oxygen	Chlorine
Test	hold a lighted splint in the mouth of the test tube	hold a glowing splint in the mouth of the test tube (light the splint, then blow it out so that the end is just glowing)	hold a piece of damp blue litmus paper in the mouth of the test tube
Result	if the gas is hydrogen, it will explode with a squeaky 'pop'	if the gas is oxygen the splint will relight (burst into flame) again	if the gas is chlorine the paper will turn red and then turn white

Worked example

A student tests a gas by holding a piece of damp blue litmus paper in it for a few seconds. The paper turns red. Student X says this proves the gas is chlorine. Student Y says the gas may be chlorine. Explain who is correct.

Student Y is correct. Chlorine is not the only gas that turns blue litmus paper red.

EXAM ALERT!

If an exam question asks how you would test something always describe the results of a test for a gas, as well as describing how to do the test.

Students have struggled with this topic in recent exams – **be prepared!** Results Plus

Many gases will turn damp blue litmus paper red. However, it is *only* chlorine that then bleaches it so that it turns white.

Now try this

target
G-D

1. Name the gases produced by the electrolysis of:
    (a) water **(1 mark)**
    (b) hydrochloric acid. **(1 mark)**

2. Name the gas that will:
    (a) relight a glowing splint **(1 mark)**
    (b) 'pop' when a lighted splint is put into it. **(1 mark)**

Ores

Some metals are found as elements in the Earth's crust. This means the metal is not combined with other elements. Metals found as elements are very unreactive metals such as gold. This means lumps of gold can sometimes be found.

Extracting metals

Most metals are found as part of a compound. For example, iron is found as iron oxide. The metal compounds are mixed up with other compounds in rocks. If a rock has enough of the metal compound to make it worthwhile to extract it, the rock is called an ore.

Metals are extracted from the compounds found in ores. The method used to extract a metal depends on how reactive the metal is.

Iron and aluminium

Metals such as iron are extracted from their compounds by heating the ores with carbon.

iron oxide + carbon
→ iron + carbon dioxide

More reactive metals such as aluminium are extracted by melting the ore and then carrying out electrolysis (see page 47). Electrolysis decomposes aluminium oxide.

aluminium oxide → aluminium + oxygen

Reactivity series

You don't need to learn the order of the elements in the table. You DO need to remember how iron and aluminium are extracted, and that the method depends on the reactivity of the metal. You should also be able to comment on how the way a metal is extracted is linked to the cost of the metal.

most reactive
(hardest and most
expensive to extract)

least reactive
(easiest and
cheapest to extract)

metal	extraction
potassium	
sodium	electrolysis of a molten compound
calcium	
magnesium	
aluminium	
zinc	
iron	
tin	heat an ore with carbon
lead	
copper	
silver	
gold	found as the uncombined element
platinum	

Worked example

A student mixes powdered charcoal (a form of carbon) with some copper oxide. After heating the mixture she finds tiny pieces of copper metal.

Explain which of these metals cannot be extracted from their compounds using the same method:

tin   aluminium   magnesium   lead

Aluminium and magnesium cannot be extracted using carbon, because they are too reactive.

Now try this

1. Name three metals that can be found in the Earth's crust as elements. **(1 mark)**

2. Explain which costs most to extract from its ore: magnesium or tin?
(3 marks)

3. Cassiterite is an ore containing tin oxide.
(a) State how the tin is extracted from cassiterite. **(1 mark)**
(b) Write a word equation to show the reaction. **(2 marks)**

Oxidation and reduction

Oxidation

Most metals react with oxygen in the air. Sometimes water also takes part in the reaction. This causes corrosion. For example, iron corrodes to form iron oxide.

iron + oxygen → iron oxide

This is an example of an oxidation reaction. The iron has been oxidised, because it has gained oxygen.

Watch out! Many metals corrode. When iron corrodes we call it rusting. Rusting only applies to iron. It is not correct to say that copper or lead 'go rusty'.

Reduction

Many metal ores contain oxides of the metal (see page 48). The metal is extracted from its compound by removing the oxygen.

aluminium oxide → aluminium + oxygen

This is an example of a reduction reaction. The aluminium oxide has been reduced, because oxygen has been removed from it.

Remember: reduction is removing oxygen.

Worked example

Explain how oxidation and reduction can happen in the same reaction. Use the word equation for the extraction of iron as an example.

You need to learn the word equations for the extraction of iron and the extraction of aluminium.

The word equation for the extraction of iron from iron oxide is:

iron oxide + carbon → iron + carbon dioxide

The iron oxide is reduced in this reaction, because oxygen is removed from it. The carbon is oxidised in the reaction.

Reactivity and corrosion

most reactive → least reactive

K	Na	Ca	Mg	Al	Zn	Fe	Sn	Pb	Cu	Ag	Au	Pt

fastest corrosion   slowest corrosion   silver, gold and platinum do not corrode at all

least resistant   more resistant   they are most resistant
to corrosion   to corrosion   to corrosion

Now try this

1. State whether these reactions are examples of oxidation or reduction:
   (a) extracting iron from iron oxide **(1 mark)**
   (b) magnesium corroding. **(1 mark)**

2. Explain which metal is more resistant to corrosion: lead or zinc. **(2 marks)**

3. Write a word equation to show the oxidation of copper. **(2 marks)**

Recycling metals

When a metal object has reached the end of its life, the metal can be melted down and made into something new so it can be used again. The metal is recycled. Recycling metals instead of throwing them away has many benefits.

 Recycling metals means the Earth's supply of metals will last longer.

 If metals are recycled, we need fewer mines. This helps the environment, because mining causes dust and noise pollution, and damages the landscape.

 Recycling produces less pollution. Extracting some ores (such as lead) can produce sulfur dioxide. This does not happen when the metal is recycled.

 Less land is needed for landfill sites.

 Carbon dioxide is emitted when fossil fuels are used to heat ores or to generate the electricity used in electrolysis. Far less carbon dioxide is emitted by the recycling process, as less energy is needed. Carbon dioxide is a greenhouse gas (you will learn more about climate change on page 59).

 For most metals, it takes less energy to melt down used metals than it does to extract the metal from its ore. This makes some recycled metals more sustainable and cheaper.

Not all metals are suitable for recycling. For some metals it costs more to collect, sort and transport the used items than is saved by recycling them.

Worked example

Look at the bar chart. State the metal that has the highest percentage recycling figure in the UK.

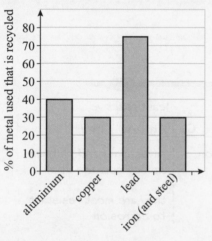

Lead

> You do not need to remember the information on the bar chart. You DO need to be able to describe what a bar chart is showing you.

Now try this

target **D-C**

1. Explain why not all metals are recycled. **(2 marks)**

2. Describe two ways in which recycling lead can reduce pollution in the atmosphere. **(4 marks)**

Properties of metals

All metals conduct heat and electricity. They are malleable (can be hammered into shape) and ductile (can be stretched into wires).

Alloys

An alloy is a mixture of metals, and sometimes carbon. Steel is an alloy made by mixing iron with small amounts of other metals and some carbon. Steel is stronger than iron, and more resistant to corrosion.

Worked example

Use the diagrams to help you to explain why alloys are generally stronger than pure metals.

In a pure metal the layers of atoms can slide over each other. An alloy is stronger because the different sized atoms jam up the structure and stop the layers from sliding.

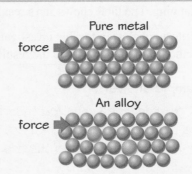

Pure metal

force

An alloy

force

Uses of metals

Not all metals have exactly the same properties. The uses of a particular metal depend on its properties.

Used for: jewellery because it looks attractive and does not corrode

some electrical connections inside electronic devices because it is one of the best electrical conductors (it is too expensive to use for cables)

Used for: bridges, cars and buildings, because it is strong and resistant to corrosion.

gold | steel
copper | aluminium

Used for: electrical cables because it is a very good conductor of electricity

water pipes because it does not corrode easily

> This is because copper is not very reactive.

Used for: drinks cans because it does not corrode

aeroplanes and some cars because it has a low density

> You would not get a mark in an exam if you wrote that aluminium is 'light'. You need to say that it has a low density, or that it is 'lightweight'.

Now try this

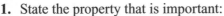

target **D-C**

1. State the property that is important:
   (a) for copper being used to make water pipes
   (b) for aluminium being used for aeroplanes
   (c) for gold being used in electronic devices.
   (3 marks)

2. Explain why steel is stronger than iron. (4 marks)

Chemistry extended writing 2

Worked example

Question 1

Jan has tested different indigestion remedies by measuring the change in pH when one tablet of each type is added to hydrochloric acid. The same amount of acid was used each time, at the same concentration and the same temperature. Each tablet was crushed up and then stirred into the acid. The pH was measured before the tablet was added. The pH changed gradually after each tablet was added. Jan wrote down the pH when it had stopped changing. The table shows Jan's results.

Write a conclusion for this investigation. Discuss how good the method was, and how good the results are. **(6 marks)**

Tablet	Change in pH	Time to reach steady pH
A	6.1	2 minutes
B	6.0	20 seconds
C	6.2	1 minute
D	5.9	3 minutes

Sample answer 1

All the remedies changed the pH by about the same amount, but tablet B changed the pH the fastest, so that is the best tablet. This was a fair test because the same amount of acid was used each time, so the results are good.

This is a good answer which comes to a clear conclusion about the results. The answer also identifies one factor that has been kept the same to make the test fair. However there are several other things that this student could have mentioned about how good they thought the results are and the way the results were collected.

Sample answer 2

The different tablets all made a similar change in pH. The best tablet to use would be B, because that made the change the fastest.

The test was fair because the same volume and concentration of acid was used for each tablet. However it might be difficult to make sure all the tablets were crushed up into the same size pieces, and they should all be the same to make sure the test is fair.

It might also be difficult to say how long it takes for the pH to change, if it is changing gradually. It might be better to time how long it takes each tablet to make the pH change by 4 or 5 units.

The results would be better if each tablet was tested at least three times. You could calculate an average from all the results.

This is an excellent answer. It has pointed out all the variables that were controlled, and mentioned one variable that may not have been controlled properly. Two improvements to the method have been suggested.

Now try this

1. Chlorine is a toxic gas, but has many uses. Discuss the uses and hazards of using chlorine. **(6 marks)**

If you are asked to 'discuss' something, your answer needs to include a conclusion. In this case you need to say whether or not you think the uses are more important than the hazards.

Chemistry extended writing 3

Worked example

Question 1

A group of students have some different ideas about what might cause iron to go rusty. Here are their ideas:

A Oxygen causes rusting.   **B** You need oxygen and water to make iron rust.
C You only need water for rust to form.

Explain how you could carry out an investigation to find out which hypothesis is correct. Use the information in the box to help you to design your investigation. **(6 marks)**

> Even distilled water contains dissolved oxygen. This can be removed by boiling the water. A layer of oil on top of water stops oxygen dissolving in the water. The air normally contains some water vapour. Calcium chloride powder absorbs water from the air.

Sample answer 1

Put two nails in test tubes. Fill one test tube with water. If the nail in the water tube goes rusty, that shows that water is needed for rust to form. If the one in the tube of air goes rusty, that shows that air is needed.

This is a basic answer. It does not explain how to test the three hypotheses. It will gain some marks because the student has said how the results will be interpreted.

Sample answer 2

I need three identical pieces of iron and three test tubes. I will put one piece of iron in each tube.

I will put distilled water in tube 1. The distilled water will have oxygen dissolved in it. Tube 2 will have calcium chloride powder in it as well as the iron to make sure there is no moisture in the air. I will put a bung on the tube to stop any more moisture getting in. Tube 3 will have boiled distilled water in it. Boiling the water gets rid of oxygen in the water. I will put a little oil on the top of the water and put a bung in the tube to stop any more moisture getting in.

If the iron in tube 2 goes rusty, it shows that only oxygen is needed for rusting, so hypothesis A would be correct. If the iron in tube 3 goes rusty it shows that only water is needed for rusting, so hypothesis C would be correct. If the only rust is in tube 1, it will show that both oxygen and water are needed for rusting, so hypothesis B will be correct.

This is an excellent answer. It has explained how to test for all three hypotheses, and also explained how the results will be interpreted.

Now try this

1. This apparatus can be used to electrolyse water or hydrochloric acid. Explain which gases form when each of these liquids is electrolysed, and how they can be identified.   **(6 marks)**

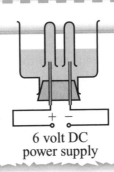

6 volt DC
power supply

Crude oil

Crude oil is a fossil fuel. It is a complex mixture of many different kinds of hydrocarbon molecules.

Hydrocarbons

Hydrocarbons are a group of compounds containing only hydrogen and carbon atoms. Each hydrocarbon molecule consists of a chain of carbon atoms surrounded by hydrogen atoms. All the atoms in each molecule are chemically joined together.

Hydrocarbons are a type of *compound*. The hydrogen and carbon atoms are chemically joined to make molecules. Students often lose marks by calling hydrocarbons a 'mixture' of carbon and hydrogen, or by saying that hydrocarbons are made of hydrogen and carbon molecules.

There are many different types of hydrocarbon, with different numbers of carbon atoms in them. The longest molecules can have hundreds of carbon atoms in them.

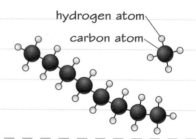

hydrogen atom

carbon atom

Worked example

Put an X in the boxes next to the two hydrocarbons.

☒ C_2H_6O ☒ C_5H_{10}
☐ C_2H_6 ☐ C_2H_5OH

Fractional distillation

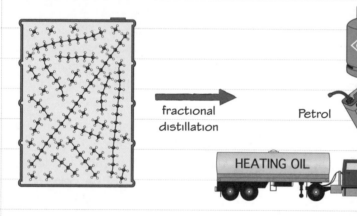

fractional distillation

Petrol

HEATING OIL

Crude oil contains a mixture of different hydrocarbon molecules. This mixture is not very useful.

These are more useful fractions. Each fraction is a simpler mixture than crude oil.

Now try this

target G-D

1. Which two statements are correct? **(2 marks)**
   A Hydrocarbons are mixtures.
   B Crude oil is a mixture of hydrocarbons. ⌐
   C Hydrocarbons are compounds. ⌣
   D Crude oil is a mixture of hydrogen and oxygen.

target D-C

2. (a) Give the name of the process used to separate crude oil into fractions. **(2 marks)**
   (b) Explain why crude oil is split into fractions. **(2 marks)**

Crude oil fractions

Each fraction obtained from crude oil contains a mixture of a few different hydrocarbons.
Each fraction has different properties and different uses.

Worked example

Complete the table to show the uses of the different fractions.

Fraction	Uses
gases	heating and cooking in homes
petrol	fuel for cars
kerosene	fuel for aircraft
diesel oil	fuel for some cars and trains
fuel oil	fuel for large ships and in some power stations
bitumen	surfacing roads and roofs

You need to remember the names of the different fractions, and their uses.

The properties of the different fractions change gradually, in the order shown in the table above. You need to remember the order of the fractions, as well as their names.

Properties

Property	Gas		Bitumen
number of carbon and hydrogen atoms in the molecules	smallest number of atoms in molecules	→	lots of atoms in each molecule
boiling point	low boiling point (gases at room temperature)	→	high boiling point (liquids at room temperature)
ignition	easy to set alight	→	difficult to set alight
viscosity	runny (low viscosity)	→	thick and sticky (high viscosity)

Now try this

Target D–G

1. Name two fractions that can be used as fuel for cars. **(2 marks)**

2. State which fraction is used as fuel for ships. **(1 mark)**

3. State which fraction:
   (a) has the lowest viscosity
   (b) has the highest boiling point
   (c) is the easiest to set alight. **(3 marks)**

Combustion

The scientific name for burning is combustion. When hydrocarbons burn they combine with oxygen to produce carbon dioxide and water. The reaction releases energy.

Combustion of methane

Methane is a hydrocarbon. It is the main gas in natural gas.

methane (CH_4) + oxygen (O_2) → carbon dioxide (CO_2) + water (H_2O)

The methane has been oxidised. Combustion is an example of an oxidation reaction.

Students often forget that water is produced when hydrocarbons burn. You can't normally see the water because the heat of the reaction means it is produced as a gas.

Complete combustion

A combustion reaction is described as complete combustion if all the hydrocarbon is oxidised and the only products are carbon dioxide and water. Complete combustion happens when there is plenty of oxygen available.

If there is not enough oxygen available, then incomplete combustion occurs (see opposite page).

Worked example

Label the diagram and use it to help you to explain the test for carbon dioxide.

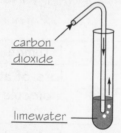

carbon dioxide

limewater

When carbon dioxide is bubbled through limewater, the carbon dioxide combines with the limewater to form solid calcium carbonate. This makes the limewater turn milky.

EXAM ALERT!

This is a good answer because it explains the test and the result you will see if the gas is carbon dioxide.

Don't say that you can test for carbon dioxide by seeing if the gas will put out a lighted splint. Carbon dioxide will put out a lighted splint, but lots of other gases do this too so it is NOT a good test for carbon dioxide.

Students have struggled with exam questions similar to this - **be prepared!** Results**Plus**

Now try this

target
G-D

1. (a) Ethane is a hydrocarbon that is part of the gases fraction from crude oil. Write a word equation for the complete combustion of ethane. **(4 marks)**
   (b) State which substance is oxidised in this reaction. **(1 mark)**

2. A reaction produces a gas that you think is carbon dioxide.
   (a) Describe how you would test the gas. **(2 marks)**
   (b) State what you would see if the gas is carbon dioxide. **(1 mark)**

Incomplete combustion

In complete combustion, all the carbon atoms in a hydrocarbon are oxidised to form carbon dioxide. All the hydrogen atoms that were in the hydrocarbon are oxidised to form water.

Incomplete combustion

Sometimes there is not enough oxygen available to allow all these oxidation reactions to take place. When incomplete combustion takes place all the hydrogen atoms become oxidised to form water, but the carbon atoms may form:

- some carbon dioxide (CO_2)
- some carbon monoxide (CO)
- some soot (particles of solid carbon).

Different amounts of these substances are produced, depending on how much oxygen is available.

> Don't forget that water is always formed when hydrocarbons burn.

methane + oxygen → carbon dioxide + carbon monoxide + carbon + water

Incomplete combustion reactions release energy.

Cars and boilers

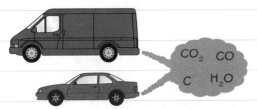

There is always incomplete combustion in vehicle engines.

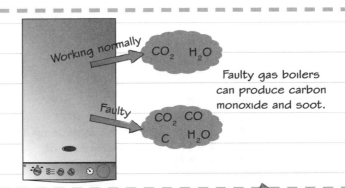

Faulty gas boilers can produce carbon monoxide and soot.

Worked example

Explain the problems caused by:
(a) carbon monoxide   **(b)** soot.

(a) Carbon monoxide is a toxic gas. It reduces the amount of oxygen that the blood can carry around the body. Breathing in carbon monoxide can kill you.

(b) Soot can:
- build up in chimneys and eventually cause fires
- cause lung diseases
- make buildings dirty.

> Dirty marks around gas appliances show that soot is being formed. This shows that incomplete combustion is taking place. Carbon monoxide may also be forming, but the soot does not directly show that this is happening.

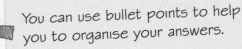

> You can use bullet points to help you to organise your answers.

Now try this

target G-D

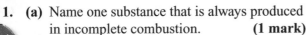

1. **(a)** Name one substance that is always produced in incomplete combustion. **(1 mark)**
   (b) Name three other substances that may be produced in incomplete combustion. **(2 marks)**

2. Explain why carbon monoxide harms the body. **(2 marks)**

3. Describe one way in which soot can cause problems. **(1 mark)**

Acid rain

Sulfur dioxide

Most hydrocarbon fuels contain impurities such as sulfur. When the hydrocarbons burn, the sulfur is oxidised to form sulfur dioxide.

Liquid hydrocarbon fuels such as petrol and diesel contain sulfur. Coal also contains sulfur. Natural gas and the gases produced from crude oil do not contain sulfur.

Sulfur dioxide dissolves in water and makes the water acidic.

Explain what acid rain is and how is it formed.

Rain water is naturally slightly acidic because it contains dissolved carbon dioxide and other acidic gases normally in the air. Acid rain is rain that is more acidic than normal because sulfur dioxide has dissolved in it.

Acid rain has a lower pH than normal rain.

The effects of acid rain

sulfur dioxide dissolves in water in the air

waste gases from power stations and vehicles contain sulfur dioxide

acid rain speeds up the weathering of buildings and statues

rain is more acidic than normal

trees are damaged

rivers, lakes and soils are more acidic, which harms organisms living in them

EXAM ALERT!

Cleaning up

The problem of acid rain is being reduced in Europe and North America by:

- removing sulfur from petrol, diesel and fuel oil
- removing acidic gases from power station emissions.

Make sure you read all the information in a question carefully. A recent exam question asked how passing waste gases from power stations through calcium carbonate helps to reduce the amount of acid rain. Many students said that the calcium carbonate was added to the clouds, even though the question told them how the calcium carbonate was used!

Students have struggled with this topic in recent exams – **be prepared!**   Results**Plus**

Now try this

target
G-D

1. (a) Name two gases that dissolve in rain water and make it acidic. **(2 marks)**

   (b) State which of these gases is responsible for making rain more acidic than normal.
   (1 mark)

2. Describe three effects of acid rain. **(3 marks)**

Climate change

Keeping warm

The Earth is warmed by the Sun, and loses heat to space. Some of the gases in the atmosphere trap heat and help to keep the Earth warm. These gases are carbon dioxide, methane and water vapour. Without these gases the average temperature on Earth would be about −18°C. These gases are sometimes called 'greenhouse gases'.

Carbon dioxide

The temperature of the Earth varies naturally over long periods of time. The amount of carbon dioxide in the atmosphere also varies naturally, and this is linked with the temperature changes.

Since 1800 the proportion of carbon dioxide in the atmosphere has increased because humans have been burning fossil fuels and so releasing carbon dioxide into the atmosphere. Farming also adds methane to the atmosphere. The graph below shows that the Earth's temperature and the concentration of carbon dioxide have both risen. This warming is called climate change.

Worked example

Evaluate how far the graph provides evidence for climate change.

The graph provides evidence that the mean world temperature has been increasing since about 1950. It also shows that the concentration of carbon dioxide has been increasing since 1850. There is a correlation between these two things, but this does not prove that increasing carbon dioxide levels are causing the warming.

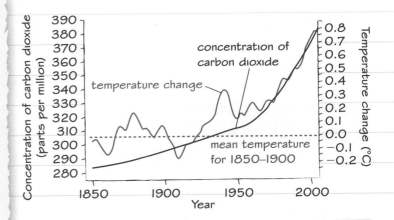

A correlation is when two quantities increase (or decrease) together. A correlation shows that the two things may be related, but it does not prove that one change causes the other.

Most scientists agree that carbon dioxide is the main cause of global warming, but this opinion is based on computer modelling and other information, not just on graphs like this.

Reducing the CO$_2$

Chemists are trying to find ways of controlling the amount of carbon dioxide in the atmosphere. Two methods being investigated are:
- 'seeding' the oceans with iron compounds
- converting carbon dioxide into hydrocarbons that can then be used as fuels.

Now try this

target
G-D

1. Name three gases that help to keep the Earth warm. **(3 marks)**
2. Describe one way in which humans may be affecting the temperature of the Earth. **(2 marks)**
3. Describe two ways in which it may be possible to control the amount of carbon dioxide in the atmosphere. **(2 marks)**

Biofuels

Biofuels are fuels obtained from living organisms and can be used instead of fossil fuels. They are a renewable resource, because more plants can be grown to replace the ones used as fuel.

Burning biofuels

Biofuels include...

- plants grown to be burned, such as wood

- sugar cane or sugar beet, which can be converted to ethanol. This can be used instead of petrol, and reduces the demand for petrol.

Burning biofuels adds less carbon dioxide to the atmosphere than burning fossil fuels. This is because the plants that were used to make the biofuel absorbed carbon dioxide from the atmosphere when they grew.

Carbon neutrality

A carbon neutral fuel is one that does not increase the total amount of carbon dioxide in the atmosphere when it burns.

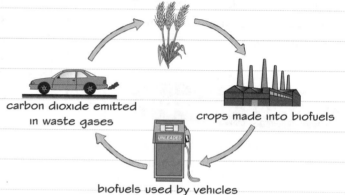

carbon dioxide absorbed in photosynthesis

crops made into biofuels

biofuels used by vehicles

carbon dioxide emitted in waste gases

Worked example

Explain why most biofuels are not carbon neutral.

When making biofuels, energy is needed to fertilise, harvest and transport the crops, and to make them into a fuel that can be used in vehicles.

At the moment this energy usually comes from burning fossil fuels, so some carbon dioxide is added to the atmosphere when the biofuels are produced.

This is a good answer because it explains why energy is needed to produce biofuels.

Advantages and disadvantages

- ✓ Biofuels are renewable.

- ✓ Biofuels add less carbon dioxide to the atmosphere than burning fossil fuels.

- ✗ Growing crops to make into biofuels means that less land is available for growing food. This leads to higher food prices and may lead to some people being short of food.

Now try this

target
G-D

1. State what is meant by a biofuel.
   (1 mark)

2. Explain why biofuels are renewable resources.
   (2 marks)

3. Describe one advantage and one disadvantage of biofuels.
   (2 marks)

Choosing fuels

Different fuels

Petrol, kerosene and diesel oil are non-renewable fossil fuels. They are all obtained from crude oil. Methane is a non-renewable fossil fuel found in natural gas.

Hydrogen is also used as a fuel. In rockets, hydrogen is burnt to release energy. Hydrogen can also be used in cars and other vehicles by using a fuel cell.

Worked example

Explain what a hydrogen fuel cell does.

A fuel cell combines hydrogen and oxygen to form water without burning. This reaction releases energy in the form of electricity.

A good fuel...

- should burn easily
- should not produce ash or smoke
- should release a lot of heat energy
- should be easy to store and transport.

Investigating fuels

If you are given a range of fuels you can work out which one gives off most heat by measuring the time taken for each fuel to raise the same volume of water by 50°C. Don't forget to measure the mass of the fuel before and after the experiment to find out how much you have used. There are lots of other variables to control such as volume of water.

Hydrogen versus petrol

Petrol	Hydrogen
✓ burns easily	✓ burns easily
✓ does not produce ash or smoke	✓ does not produce ash or smoke
✗ produces carbon dioxide and carbon monoxide as well as water when it burns	✓ only produces water when it burns
✓ releases more energy per kg when it burns than fuels such as coal or wood	✓ releases nearly three times as much energy per kg as petrol
✓ is a liquid, so it is easy to store and transport	✗ is a gas, so it has to be stored at high pressure
	✗ filling stations would need to be adapted for hydrogen to be used in cars

You may be asked to **evaluate** the advantages or disadvantages of different fuels. This means comparing the fuels and saying which one you think is best. The important thing is to **give a reason** for your conclusion.

Now try this

1. (a) Name three non-renewable fuels obtained from crude oil. **(1 mark)**
   (b) Name one fossil fuel obtained from natural gas. **(1 mark)**

2. Explain why petrol is a better fuel for cars than coal. **(2 marks)**

Alkanes

Alkanes are a group of hydrocarbon molecules. Crude oil is made of a mixture of different alkane molecules. The three simplest alkanes are methane, ethane and propane. These compounds are found in natural gas.

Methane is the main component in natural gas.

Saturated hydrocarbons

Alkanes all consist of a chain of carbon atoms bonded together. Each carbon atom is also bonded to two or three hydrogen atoms.

Alkanes are saturated hydrocarbons. This means that all the bonds joining carbon atoms to each other are single bonds.

Naming alkanes

The names of all alkanes end in '-ane'. The first part of the name of an alkane tells you the number of carbon atoms in each molecule.

- Methane (CH_4) has only one carbon atom.
- Ethane (C_2H_6) has two carbon atoms.
- Propane (C_3H_8) has three carbon atoms.

You need to learn the formulae of the first three alkanes, and you need to be able to draw their structures. You can just represent each atom using a letter, as shown in the diagrams on this page.

You also need to learn what the 'meth', 'eth' and 'prop' mean. They mean the same thing for the alkene family of hydrocarbons.

Worked example

Draw the structures of methane, ethane and propane to show how the atoms are bonded together.

```
    H              H  H           H  H  H
    |              |  |           |  |  |
H — C — H      H — C — C — H  H — C — C — C — H
    |              |  |           |  |  |
    H              H  H           H  H  H

 methane          ethane            propane
```

Remember that each carbon atom bonds to four other atoms. Hydrogen atoms form only one bond.

Now try this

1. Name three alkanes that are gases.
   (3 marks)

2. Name the two elements found in alkane molecules.
   (2 marks)

3. Write down the formula of propane.
   (1 mark)

Alkenes

The alkenes are a family of hydrocarbon molecules. They are similar to alkanes, except that alkene molecules have at least one double bond between two of the carbon atoms.

You need to learn the names of the smallest two alkenes.

- Ethene (C_2H_4) has two carbon atoms.
- Propene (C_3H_6) has three carbon atoms.

> It is very easy to get alkanes and alkenes confused, as the names are very similar. Read a question very carefully to check whether the name has an a or an e in the middle!

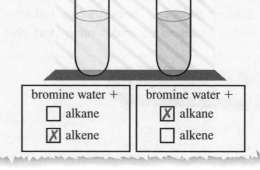

Double bonds

Alkenes are unsaturated molecules, because they include a double bond.

> Make sure that you know the meanings of these words:
> - only single bonds = saturated
> - double bond = unsaturated

The bromine test

The bromine test is used to find out if a liquid contains double bonds. Bromine water (bromine dissolved in water) is an orange solution.

> Bromine water can also be pale yellow or red-brown, depending on how much bromine is dissolved. The important thing to remember is that bromine water is coloured.

Worked example

Put a cross in the correct boxes to show which substance has been added to the bromine water in each tube, and explain your answer.

Bromine does not react with alkanes, so the colour does not change.

Bromine reacts with alkenes and changes from orange to colourless.

bromine water +	bromine water +
☐ alkane	☒ alkane
☒ alkene	☐ alkene

EXAM ALERT!

It is not correct to say 'clear'. Clear means transparent, and is not a colour. The bromine water is clear and orange. It changes to clear and colourless when a substance containing double bonds is added.

> Students have struggled with exam questions similar to this - **be prepared!**

Now try this

1. Draw the structure of a propene molecule.
   (3 marks)

2. (a) Describe two similarities between ethene and ethane. **(2 marks)**
   (b) Describe two differences. **(2 marks)**

3. Explain what you would see if you shake up bromine water with:
   (a) ethane **(2 marks)**
   (b) propene. **(2 marks)**

Cracking

Crude oil contains a mixture of long and short alkane molecules, but the short ones are the most useful. The long chains are broken down into shorter chains by cracking.

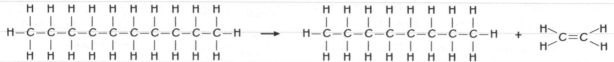

The long molecules are not very useful.

Cracking breaks down the long molecules by heating them.

Cracking produces shorter-chain alkanes, which are useful as fuels.

Cracking also produces alkenes, which are used to make polymers.

> Remember that alkanes are saturated molecules (they have only single bonds), and alkenes are unsaturated molecules (they contain a double bond).

EXAM ALERT!

Don't get fractional distillation and cracking mixed up. Fractional distillation is a physical separation process, and does not change any molecules. Cracking is a chemical reaction, and breaks down the molecules.

Students have struggled with this topic in recent exams – **be prepared!**

Cracking paraffin

Paraffin is an alkane. Liquid paraffin can be cracked in the laboratory using the apparatus shown in the diagram below.

- The porous pot is heated strongly.
- The liquid paraffin is heated and it evaporates.
- The paraffin vapour passes over the hot porous pot and the hydrocarbon molecules break down.
- One of the products is ethene, which is a gas.
- The ethene bubbles through the water and collects above the water in the other tube. The water is used to make sure that the only gas in the test tube is ethene.

Worked example

Label the diagram used for cracking paraffin in the laboratory.

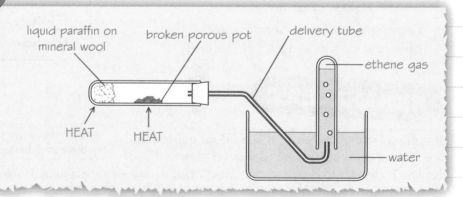

Now try this

target
G-D

1. Explain why some alkanes are cracked.
   (2 marks)

2. Suggest one safety precaution you should take when cracking paraffin in the laboratory. **(1 mark)**

target
D-C

3. Describe how you would test the gas produced by cracking liquid paraffin to find out if it contained any unsaturated molecules. **(2 marks)**

Polymerisation

Ethene molecules have a double bond between the two carbon atoms. Lots of ethene molecules can be made to join up to form one long molecule called poly(ethene). The (poly)ethene only has single bonds between carbon atoms.

[chemical structure diagram of ethene molecules]

↓ Polymerisation

[chemical structure diagram of poly(ethene)]

Other small alkene molecules can be joined up to make long molecules. The small molecules are called monomers. Lots of monomers join up to make polymers.

Worked example

Fill in the gaps to show the names of the polymers made from these monomers.

Propene monomers make _poly(propene)._

Chloroethene monomers make _poly(chloroethene)._

Tetrafluoroethene monomers make poly(tetrafluoroethene) or _PTFE._

> Poly(chloroethene) is also called PVC.

> Poly(tetrafluoroethene) is also called PTFE. You don't need to memorise 'poly(tetrafluoroethene)' - just remember the initials.

Properties and uses

Different polymers have different properties, so they have different uses.

Polymer	Properties	Uses
poly(ethene)	flexible, cheap	plastic bags, plastic bottles and clingfilm
poly(propene)	flexible, shatterproof, has a high softening point	buckets and bowls
poly(chloroethene) (PVC)	tough, cheap, long lasting, good insulator	window frames, gutters and pipes, insulation for electrical wires
PTFE	tough, slippery	non-stick coatings for frying pans and skis, stain-proofing carpets

Now try this

1. State whether each of these substances is a monomer or a polymer:
   (a) PTFE   (1 mark)
   (b) ethene.   (1 mark)

2. State which plastic (or plastics) can be used for the following purposes:
   (a) clingfilm   (1 mark)
   (b) window frames.   (1 mark)

3. PVC is used to coat electrical wires. State which property is the most important for this use.   (1 mark)

Problems with polymers

Biodegradability

Many materials we throw away are biodegradable. They eventually rot away because microbes feed on them and break them down. Most polymers are not biodegradable. This is useful, because products made from them last a long time. It is also a problem, because when polymers have been thrown away they do not rot.

> Don't get 'biodegradable' mixed up with 'corrosion'. Materials biodegrade when microbes decompose them. Materials corrode when they are attacked by chemical substances in the environment.

Disposing of polymers

Landfill sites
- polymers are not biodegradable
- they last for many years
- we are running out of landfill sites ✗

Burning ✗
- many polymers release toxic gases when they burn

Disposing of polymers

Recycling
- melting or breaking down polymers to make new objects ✓

Biodegradable polymers
- these are being developed
- they will rot away in landfill sites ✓

Worked example

Explain why recycling polymers is harder than recycling glass.

There are many different kinds of polymer. The polymer waste has to be sorted before the different polymers can be broken down or melted and made into new objects.

> Watch out! Reusing and recycling are not the same. Reusing means using the same object several times (such as using plastic carrier bags for shopping many times). Recycling means that the material is made into new objects.

Now try this

1. Most polymers are not biodegradable.
   (a) Explain what this means. **(2 marks)**
   (b) State why this is a problem when polymer materials are thrown away.
   (2 marks)

2. Describe a problem that may be caused by burning waste polymers. **(1 mark)**

3. Explain why recycling can help to solve problems with disposing of polymers.
   (2 marks)

Chemistry extended writing 4

Worked example

Biofuels are often described as 'carbon neutral'.

Explain why most biofuels available at present are not carbon neutral. Your answer should include a definition of carbon neutral. **(6 marks)**

Sample answer 1

A carbon neutral fuel does not produce carbon dioxide when it burns. Biofuels are not carbon neutral because all fuels produce carbon dioxide.

This answer would not get any marks because the science in it is incorrect. The sample answer below has the correct definition of 'carbon neutral'. Although it is true that biofuels do produce carbon dioxide when they burn, this is not true of all fuels (hydrogen, for example, only produces water when it burns).

Sample answer 2

A carbon neutral fuel does not add any carbon dioxide to the atmosphere overall. This is because biofuels are made from living things, and all living things originally get their energy from plants. The plants grew by taking carbon dioxide out of the atmosphere for photosynthesis. So when the biofuel burns it is only putting carbon dioxide into the atmosphere that the plants originally took out.

Growing plants need fertilisers, and the crops have to be harvested and taken to a factory to make into biofuels. The factory also needs energy. Most of this energy will come from burning fossil fuels in power stations or in lorry engines. Burning these fossil fuels puts carbon dioxide into the atmosphere, so using the biofuel is responsible for adding some carbon dioxide overall.

This is an excellent answer. It explains everything that the question asked, and the information is organised into a separate paragraph for each part of the question.

Now try this

1. This apparatus can be used to show the substances produced in the complete combustion of a hydrocarbon fuel.

   Explain what you would see when the fuel burns with a full supply of air and then without enough air. **(6 marks)**

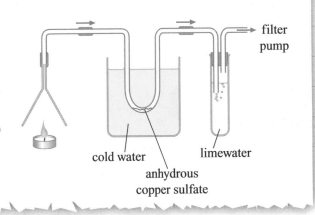

filter pump

cold water

anhydrous copper sulfate

limewater

Chemistry extended writing 5

Worked example

Alkanes and alkenes are two families of molecules. Describe the similarities and differences between alkanes and alkenes, and describe a test that can be used to tell them apart. **(6 marks)**

Sample answer 1

Alkanes are made of hydrogen and carbon molecules. Their names all end in 'ane'.

Alkenes are made of hydrogen and carbon molecules. Their names all end in 'ene'. They have double bonds between the molecules.

You can test with bromine.

This is a basic answer. There is not much information given, and some of it is incorrect (alkanes and alkenes are molecules made up of hydrogen and carbon *atoms*). Bromine water is used to test for the double bond in alkenes, and if you are asked to describe the test for a substance you should always describe the test *and* what you would see if the substance is present.

Sample answer 2

Similarities	Differences
they are both hydrocarbons (with only carbon and hydrogen atoms)	alkanes only have single bonds between the carbon atoms, but alkenes have at least one double bond
the carbon atoms in them are in long chains	alkenes can be used to make polymers, alkanes cannot
the first part of the name says how many carbon atoms there are in each molecule	alkanes are found in crude oil, but alkenes are made from crude oil by cracking long molecules
	alkenes react with bromine, alkanes do not

To test for an alkene, mix the alkene with some bromine water. The bromine water is an orange colour. If there is an alkene present the colour will disappear and the mixture will become colourless.

This is an excellent answer. A table is a good way of organising an answer that asks for similarities and differences. The description of the test for alkenes is good, because it describes what to do *and* what you would see if an alkene was present.

Now try this

1. Rainwater is naturally acidic, because some carbon dioxide from the atmosphere dissolves in it.

   Explain what acid rain is, how it is formed and why it is a problem. **(6 marks)**

The Solar System

Many early people thought that the Sun and all the planets moved around the Earth.

Changing ideas

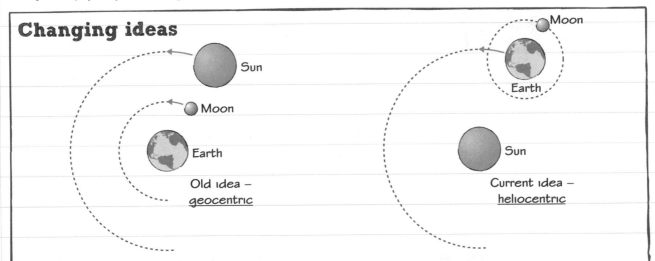

Old idea –
geocentric

Current idea –
heliocentric

In about 130 CE a Greek astronomer called Ptolemy published a geocentric ('Earth-centred') model that tried to explain the motions of the planets.

In 1543 Nicolaus Copernicus published a book that argued that the Earth and the planets were in orbits around the Sun. This is a heliocentric ('Sun-centred') model.

Ways of observing the Universe using light waves

- We can see some stars and planets using the naked eye.
- Telescopes allow us to see more distant and fainter objects, because the large objective lenses or mirrors gather more light.
- Photographs provide a record of observations that can be studied later or analysed by computer. Cameras can also record light arriving through a telescope over many minutes, so they can produce pictures of objects too dim to see just by looking through a telescope.

Galileo

Galileo Galilei was the first astronomer to make observations using telescopes. In 1610 he reported that he had observed four moons orbiting Jupiter. These were the first objects seen to be orbiting around something that was not the Earth. This observation supported Copernicus's ideas.

You don't need to remember the dates for Ptolemy, Copernicus and Galileo, but you should remember the order of the different ideas and observations.

Now try this

 target G-D

1. What is the difference between a geocentric and a heliocentric model of the Solar System?   **(2 marks)**

 target D-C

2. (a) What evidence did Galileo find that backed up Copernicus's ideas?   **(1 mark)**

   (b) Discuss how this evidence supported the heliocentric model.   **(2 marks)**

Reflection and refraction

Light travels as waves. Light normally travels in straight lines, unless it is reflected or refracted.

Worked example

Explain the difference between reflection and refraction.

Reflection happens when light bounces off a boundary between different materials. Mirrors reflect light evenly.

Refraction happens when light passes from one material to another. If light passes through the boundary between two transparent materials at an angle its direction will change.

Lenses

Lenses are specially shaped pieces of transparent material that change the direction of light rays. A converging lens makes rays of light come together.

- The point at which parallel rays are brought together is called the focal point. The distance between a lens and the focal point is called the focal length.
- The fatter the lens, the shorter the focal length.
- The magnification of the image depends on the focal length and the distance between the object and the lens.

A converging lens can be used as a magnifying glass if it is held close to an object.

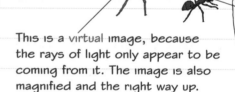

This is a virtual image, because the rays of light only appear to be coming from it. The image is also magnified and the right way up.

Finding the focal length

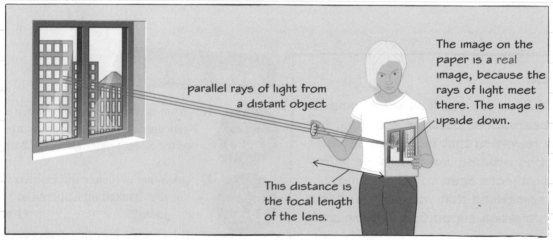

parallel rays of light from a distant object

This distance is the focal length of the lens.

The image on the paper is a real image, because the rays of light meet there. The image is upside down.

Now try this

target **G–D**

1. Do lenses make use of reflection or refraction?
(1 mark)

2. What is the focal length of a lens? **(3 marks)**

target **D–C**

3. Describe how to measure the focal length of a converging lens.
(4 marks)

Telescopes

Simple telescope

The first telescopes used lenses to gather more light and to magnify the image. A refracting telescope uses two converging lenses. The objective lens brings rays of light from a distant object to a point to form an image. The eyepiece lens acts as a magnifying glass and magnifies this image.

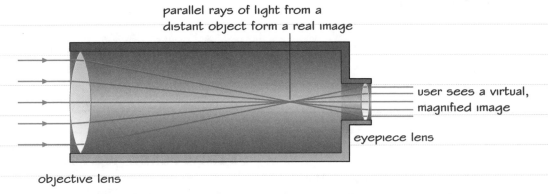

parallel rays of light from a distant object form a real image

user sees a virtual, magnified image

eyepiece lens

objective lens

Reflecting telescope

A reflecting telescope uses curved mirrors to gather light from distant objects and a converging lens as an eyepiece to magnify the image. If a telescope needs to see very dim objects, it is easier to make a very large mirror than a very large lens. Reflecting telescopes give better quality images than refracting telescopes of similar sizes.

Worked example

Complete the labels on this diagram of a reflecting telescope.

You need to be able to explain how the two different types of telescope work, but you will not be asked to draw ray diagrams.

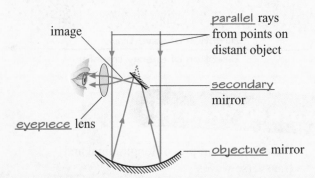

image

parallel rays from points on distant object

secondary mirror

eyepiece lens

objective mirror

The eyepiece lens magnifies the image produced by the mirrors.

Now try this

target D-C

1. Which kind of telescope uses:
   (a) mirrors and lenses   **(1 mark)**
   (b) only lenses?   **(1 mark)**

target D-B

2. Which part of these telescopes is responsible for magnifying the image?
   (a) a simple telescope   **(1 mark)**
   (b) a reflecting telescope.   **(1 mark)**

Waves

Waves transfer energy and information without transferring matter.

Describing waves

Waves can be described by their

- frequency – the number of waves passing a point each second, measured in hertz (Hz)
- speed – measured in metres per second (m/s)
- wavelength and amplitude

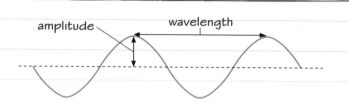

Watch out! Remember that the amplitude is *half* of the distance from the top to the bottom of the wave. Students often get this wrong.

Longitudinal waves

Sound waves are longitudinal waves. The particles in the material the sound is travelling through move back and forth along the same direction that the sound is travelling.

Particles in a longitudinal wave move along the same direction as the wave.

longitudinal wave

air particles move like this

direction of wave travel
direction of energy transfer

Transverse waves

Waves on a water surface are transverse waves. The particles of water move in a direction at right angles to the direction the wave is travelling.

water particles move like this

transverse wave

direction of wave travel
direction of energy transfer

Particles in a transverse wave move across the direction the wave is travelling.

Worked example

State some examples of longitudinal and transverse waves.

You will learn more about seismic waves on page 87.

Longitudinal waves: sound waves and seismic P waves.

Transverse waves: waves on water, electromagnetic waves, seismic S waves.

Now try this

target
G-D

1. What are the correct units for these quantities:
   (a) wavelength **(1 mark)**
   (b) speed **(1 mark)**
   (c) frequency? **(1 mark)**

2. (a) Sketch a transverse wave and mark the amplitude and wavelength on it. **(3 marks)**
   (b) Draw an arrow to show which way the wave moves. **(1 mark)**
   (c) Draw a small particle on the wave, with arrows to show which way it moves. **(1 mark)**

Wave equations

You may need to use one of these equations in your exam.

Speed, frequency and wavelength

$v = f \times \lambda$ v = wave speed
                (metres per second, m/s)
         f = frequency (hertz, Hz)
         λ = wavelength (metres, m)

λ is the Greek letter 'lambda'.

Speed, distance and time

$v = \dfrac{x}{t}$ v = wave speed
              (metres/second, m/s)
       x = distance (metres, m)
       t = time (seconds, s)

Worked example

A seismic wave has a frequency of 15 Hz and a wavelength of 270 m. Calculate the speed of the wave.

$v = f \times \lambda$
$ = 15\,\text{Hz} \times 270\,\text{m}$
$ = 4050\,\text{m/s}$

Choose the equation that includes frequency and wavelength.

Worked example

A wave on the sea takes 5 seconds to travel along a 20 m long pier. Calculate the speed of the wave.

$v = \dfrac{x}{t}$
$ = \dfrac{20\,\text{m}}{5\,\text{s}}$
$ = 4\,\text{m/s}$

You do not need to remember the equations. They will be provided on a formula sheet in your exam. But you do need to be able to choose the correct equation to use, and to use the correct units.

EXAM ALERT!

Always show your working in calculation questions. Even if your final answer is wrong you may have used the right method.

Students have struggled with exam questions similar to this - **be prepared!** ResultsPlus

Now try this

1. A sound wave with a frequency of 100 Hz has a wavelength of 3.3 m. Calculate the speed of the wave.

(3 marks)

2. A wave in the sea travels 1500 m in one minute (60 seconds). Calculate the speed of the wave.

(3 marks)

Beyond the visible

The light we can see with our eyes is visible light. Light can be split up into the seven colours of the visible spectrum. Visible light is part of a 'family' of electromagnetic waves (see opposite page).

The colours of the visible spectrum are...

Red	Orange	Yellow	Green	Blue	Indigo	Violet

longest wavelength
lowest frequency

shortest wavelength
highest frequency

> Remember the order of the colours by remembering the name Roy G Biv.

Herschel and infrared

William Herschel **discovered** infrared radiation.

He used a prism to split light into the colours of the visible spectrum.

He used a thermometer to investigate the heating effect from each colour.

The heating increased from violet to red.

He investigated the region beyond the red.

He found an even bigger heating effect. He had discovered infrared radiation.

> 'Infra' means 'below'. Infrared radiation is 'below' visible red light because it has a longer wavelength and lower frequency.

Ritter and ultraviolet

Worked example

Explain how Johann Ritter discovered ultraviolet radiation.

Ritter used a chemical called silver chloride, which turns black when light shines on it. Silver chloride turns black faster in violet light than it does in red light. It turned black even faster when it was exposed to invisible radiation beyond the violet part of the spectrum. Ritter had discovered ultraviolet radiation.

> When you are asked to explain a contribution that someone makes to science you need to explain what they did and then what they discovered.

> 'Ultra' means 'above'. Ultraviolet radiation is 'above' visible violet light because it has a shorter wavelength and higher frequency.

Now try this

1. Which colour of the visible spectrum has:
   (a) the lowest frequency? **(1 mark)**
   (b) the shortest wavelength? **(1 mark)**

2. Explain the effect on a thermometer of putting it into the ultraviolet part of the spectrum compared to the visible part of the spectrum. **(3 marks)**

The electromagnetic spectrum

Infrared radiation, visible light and ultraviolet radiation are all part of the electromagnetic spectrum.

All electromagnetic waves...

- are transverse waves (the electromagnetic vibrations are at right angles to the direction the wave is travelling – see page 72)
- travel at the same speed in a vacuum.

Watch out! The different parts of the electromagnetic spectrum have different properties, which you will read about on the following pages. But it is important to remember that some of their properties are *the same*. They are *all* transverse waves, and *all* travel at the same speed in a vacuum.

The electromagnetic spectrum

The electromagnetic spectrum is a group of waves that have different wavelengths and frequencies that are part of a continuous spectrum. Scientists put the waves into different groups according to their properties.

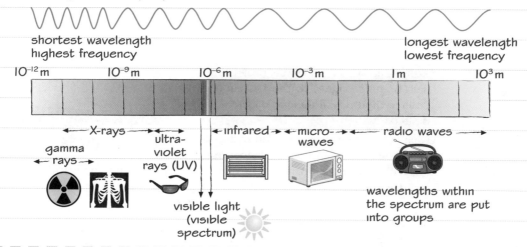

Worked example

List the parts of the electromagnetic spectrum, starting with the longest wavelength waves.

radio waves, microwaves, infrared, visible light, ultraviolet, X-rays, gamma rays

You can use a mnemonic to help you to remember the order. A mnemonic is a sentence or phrase whose words have the same initial letters as the list you are trying to remember. For example: Red Monkeys In Vans Use X-ray Glasses

Now try this

target
G-D

1. Write down three parts of the electromagnetic spectrum with shorter wavelengths than visible light.   **(3 marks)**

2. Which waves in the electromagnetic spectrum have:
   (a) the highest frequency?   **(1 mark)**
   (b) the longest wavelength?   **(1 mark)**

3. Write down two properties that *all* electromagnetic waves have.   **(2 marks)**

Electromagnetic dangers

All electromagnetic waves transfer energy. The amount of energy transferred depends on the frequency of the wave. The higher the frequency, the more energy the wave transfers.

Worked example

The energy transferred by electromagnetic waves can harm living things.

Explain why the potential danger from X-rays and gamma rays is greater than the danger from lower-frequency waves.

X-rays and gamma rays have the highest frequencies. The higher the frequency, the more energy the wave transfers and the more harm it can do.

Remember: higher frequency = more energy = more harmful.

highest
frequency
highest
energy

gamma rays	X-rays and gamma rays can cause mutations (changes) to the DNA in cells in the body. This may kill the cells or cause cancer.
X-rays	
ultraviolet	UV in sunlight can damage skin cells, causing sunburn. Over time, exposure to UV can cause skin cancer. UV can also damage the eyes.
visible light	
infrared	Infrared radiation transfers heat energy. Too much infrared radiation can cause skin burns.
microwaves	Microwaves heat water – so they can heat the water inside our bodies. Heating cells can damage or kill them.
radio waves	

lowest
frequency
lowest
energy

EXAM ALERT!

Make sure you learn the order of the waves, and the uses and harmful effects of each type of wave.

Students have struggled with this topic in recent exams – **be prepared!**

Now try this

target
G-D

1. Why are microwaves less harmful than ultraviolet radiation?   **(2 marks)**

2. Name all the parts of the electromagnetic spectrum that:
   (a) can cause cancer   **(1 mark)**
   (b) cause damage by heating   **(1 mark)**
   (c) are particularly dangerous to the eyes.   **(1 mark)**

This question has 2 marks, so you need to include two ideas in your answer.

Using electromagnetic radiation

Different parts of the electromagnetic spectrum have different uses, which depend on their properties.

Radio waves are used...

- to broadcast radio and TV programmes
- to communicate with ships, aeroplanes and satellites.

Microwaves are used...

- in mobile phones, and to communicate with satellites
- for cooking (in microwave ovens).

Microwaves cook food from the inside. Food cooked using microwaves does not go brown. Infrared cooks food from the outside, and the outside goes brown.

Infrared radiation is used...

- in cooking (by grills and toasters)
- to make thermal images (images using heat), used by police and rescue services
- in short-range communications, such as between laptops or other small computers
- in remote controls for TVs and other appliances, where the signal only has to travel short distances
- to send information along optical fibres
- in security systems such as burglar alarms, to detect people moving around.

Worked example

Describe three uses for visible light.

Visible light allows us to see. It is used to light up rooms, buildings and roads. It is used in photography.

Ultraviolet (UV) radiation is used...

- to detect security marks made using special pens
- in fluorescent lamps
- to detect forged banknotes (real banknotes have markings that glow in UV light)
- to disinfect water.

X-rays are used...

- to look inside objects, including human bodies
- in airport security scanners, to see what people have in their luggage.

Gamma rays are used...

- to sterilise food and medical equipment
- in scanners to detect cancer
- to treat cancer.

Now try this

target G-D

1. For each of these people, state which parts of the electromagnetic spectrum they may use, and how they may use them:
   (a) cooks (2 marks)
   (b) security guards or the police (3 marks)
   (c) doctors and hospitals. (2 marks)

2. Describe how three different types of electromagnetic waves are used in communications. (3 marks)

Ionising radiation

Effects of ionisation

The energy transferred by ionising radiation can remove electrons from atoms to form ions. Ions are very reactive and can cause mutations to the DNA in cells. This can lead to cancer. Too much ionising radiation can kill cells, which is why gamma rays are useful for sterilising surgical instruments.

Radioactive sources

Some elements are radioactive. These elements naturally emit ionising radiation all the time. This ionising radiation can be alpha (α) particles, beta (β) particles or gamma (γ) rays. All forms of ionising radiation transfer energy.

Worked example

Complete the table showing the properties of different types of ionising radiation.

Radiation	Particles or waves?
alpha	particles
beta	particles
gamma	waves

It is important to remember which kinds of ionising radiations are particles and which are waves. Use this completed table to help you.

Safe working

Substances that emit ionising radiation have hazard symbols on their containers. Laboratories or other places where these substances are used may also have hazard symbols. The symbols show people the dangers from the substances. People can also use the symbols to look up the safe working procedures for using the substances.

You do not need to learn the different hazard symbols, but you do need to be able to explain why hazard symbols are used.

Now try this

target G–D

1. Write down the types of ionising radiation:
   (a) that are electromagnetic waves **(1 mark)**
   (b) that are particles. **(1 mark)**

target D–B

2. (a) Explain why ionising radiation is dangerous. **(4 marks)**
   (b) Explain how hazard symbols help to reduce the dangers. **(2 marks)**

Physics extended writing 1

To answer an extended writing question successfully you need to:

✓ use your scientific knowledge to answer the question

✓ organise your answer so that it is logical and well ordered

✓ use full sentences in your writing and make sure that your spelling, punctuation and grammar are correct.

Worked example

X-rays have many uses, but they can also cause harm. Discuss whether the benefits of X-rays outweigh the risks. **(6 marks)**

Sample answer 1

X-rays are used to find broken bones and used for security. This is important. X-rays are harmful because they cause cancer.

This is a basic answer. The answer describes two uses of X-rays, but it does not explain them. Saying that X-rays are 'used for security' is too vague. This does not actually answer the question by saying whether or not the benefits outweigh the risks.

Sample answer 2

X-rays can be used to look at the insides of objects because they pass through many materials that visible light does not. X-rays can be used to look for broken bones or other medical problems. X-rays are also used in airport scanners to check inside luggage for dangerous items.

X-rays can be dangerous because they can cause damage to cells in the body and cause mutations in DNA. This can lead to cancer.

X-rays are safe if they are used with proper precautions, so I think the benefits outweigh the risks.

This is an excellent answer, because it describes and explains some of the uses, and also describes the dangers. The answer gives the student's conclusion, which is important when the question asks for an opinion.

Now try this

1. The drawing shows a reflecting telescope. Alex is making a model of this telescope using a curved mirror, a plane (flat) mirror and a lens.

   Explain how these items can be arranged to make a reflecting telescope, and why the telescope produces a virtual image.

   (6 marks)

The Universe

The Earth is one of eight planets that orbit around the Sun. The Sun is a star. Some of the planets have moons orbiting around them. The Sun, the planets and their moons all make up the Solar System.

Worked example

Explain the meanings of the words 'galaxy' and 'Universe'.

A galaxy is a collection of millions of stars. The Sun is part of a galaxy called the Milky Way. All the stars we can see in the sky at night are in the Milky Way.

There are billions of other galaxies. All the galaxies make up the Universe.

You need to remember the meanings of key words such as galaxy, Milky Way and Universe.

Watch out! A 'moon' (with no capital letter) means something orbiting around one of the other planets in the Solar System. The Moon (with a capital letter) is the object orbiting around the Earth.

Relative distances

In order of distance from Earth, starting with the closest:

Moon → Sun → planets in the Solar System → other stars → other galaxies

Earth   Moon

You could fit 30 'Earths' between the Earth and Moon.

Sun – over 11 000 'Earths' away →

Most of the planets are always further away from the Earth than the Sun. Mercury, Venus and Mars are sometimes closer.

Relative sizes

In order of size, starting with the smallest:

Moon → Earth → planets → the Sun and other stars → galaxies → Universe

Jupiter, Saturn, Uranus and Neptune are all much bigger than the Earth, Venus is about the same size, and Mercury and Mars are smaller.

You need to be able to compare the relative sizes of different things in the Universe, and also the distances between them.

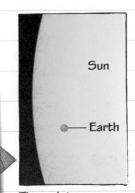

Sun

Earth

The relative sizes of the Earth and the Sun

Now try this

target
G-D

1. Write down a definition of the Solar System. **(1 mark)**

2. State which is the smallest: a star or a moon. **(1 mark)**

3. State which is furthest from the Earth: Sirius (a star in the Milky Way) or Neptune. **(1 mark)**

Exploring the Universe

Modern telescopes

The first scientists explored the Universe by observing the visible light emitted by stars. They made more discoveries after telescopes were invented. Modern telescopes are very different to the early telescopes.

Development	Impact
greater magnifications	we can observe galaxies that are far away
recording observations using photography or digital cameras	we can gather more data
can be made with greater precision	we get clearer images

The electromagnetic spectrum

Today, scientists also explore the Universe using other parts of the electromagnetic spectrum (see page 75). Some objects in space emit more X-rays, ultraviolet, infrared or radio waves than visible light. By observing these waves scientists have discovered objects that they could not have detected using visible light.

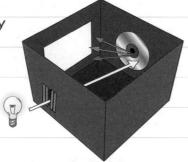

You can split the visible part of the electromagnetic spectrum into its different colours using a simple spectrometer made with a CD or DVD. The black lines are formed because some wavelengths of light will be absorbed by the Sun's atmosphere.

Telescopes in space

Some parts of the electromagnetic spectrum are absorbed by the Earth's atmosphere. Telescopes used to observe infrared, ultraviolet, X-rays and gamma rays must be put on satellites in space.

Ground-based telescopes observe visible light and radio waves.

radio telescopes detect radio waves　optical telescopes detect visible light

Telescopes in many places on Earth also suffer from light pollution, where light from streetlights and other sources makes it difficult to see the stars.

EXAM ALERT!

This is a good answer because it mentions two different reasons why some visible light telescopes are put into space, and also describes the effect of each factor.

Students have struggled with exam questions similar to this – **be prepared!**　ResultsPlus

Worked example

The Hubble Space Telescope produces images using visible light. Why are some telescopes that observe visible light put into space?

Telescopes for visible light do not have to be in space because visible light can pass through the atmosphere. But the atmosphere contains dust and clouds, which can block the view of the stars. The atmosphere can also distort images and make them less clear.

Now try this

 target G-D

1. Name three parts of the electromagnetic spectrum that can be detected by space telescopes but not by Earth-based ones. **(3 marks)**

 target D-C

2. Explain why an X-ray telescope must be put onto a satellite. **(2 marks)**

Alien life?

The Earth is the only planet where we know that life exists. Scientists look for signs of life on other planets in several different ways.

Signs of life

 Life on Earth depends on liquid water. If there are signs that other planets have liquid water, then it is possible that life may exist there.

Plants on the Earth release oxygen during photosynthesis. Scientists can look for oxygen in the atmospheres of other planets, which may indicate life.

METHANE Living organisms take in chemical substances as food and release other materials as waste. If one of these chemical changes is detected, it may be a sign of life.

Looking for the signs

Space probes can fly past planets or go into orbit around them. The probes can take images of other planets in the Solar System and send the information back to Earth.

Landers and rovers also investigate the surfaces of planets or moons. They can take close-up images, and test soil samples for microbes or for substances indicating life. A lander stays in one place on the planet, but a rover can move around.

This rover explored part of the surface of Mars.

Intelligent life?

If there is intelligent life on other planets, the 'aliens' may be trying to contact us using radio waves.

Watch out! Electromagnetic waves can travel through the vacuum of space. Sound waves *cannot* travel in a vacuum. Scientists are not looking for sound waves from alien civilisations. They are looking for radio waves.

Worked example

Explain what SETI is.

SETI stands for the Search for Extraterrestrial Intelligence. Information gathered by radio telescopes is analysed to see if there are any patterns in it, which could be a sign of intelligent life.

Now try this

 target G-D

1. Name one gas and one liquid that scientists look for to see if there might be life on another planet. **(2 marks)**

target E-D

2. Describe two things that a lander on Mars could do that cannot be done from an orbiter. **(2 marks)**

 target D-C

3. Explain how testing soil samples might show that life exists. **(2 marks)**

Life-cycles of stars

The Sun formed about 4.5 billion years ago, and will last about another 5.5 billion years before it changes into a red giant. All stars that have a similar mass to the Sun go through the same stages in their life-cycle.

> The life-cycle of a star is not like the life-cycle of a living organism. Stars do not reproduce.

A nebula is a cloud of dust and gas. The gas is mostly hydrogen. The dust and gas can be pulled together by gravity. The hydrogen gets hotter as it spirals inwards and gravitational potential energy is converted to thermal energy.

> It is important to remember that the force of gravity pulls the nebula together to make a star.

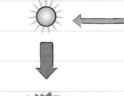

Eventually the gas gets hot enough for the nuclei of hydrogen atoms in the gas cloud to fuse together. Fusion reactions turn hydrogen atoms into helium and release a lot of energy. The star begins to shine. This stage of a star's life-cycle is called the main sequence. The Sun is a main sequence star.

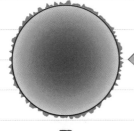

After about 10 billion years the star will have used up most of its hydrogen fuel. When this happens it swells up to become a red giant. Other elements fuse together in the collapsing core of the red giants.

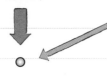

Eventually all the elements that can take part in nuclear fusion reactions are used up. Fusion reactions in the star stop. Gravity pulls the material together to make a much smaller white dwarf star. The star gradually cools down.

> Stars take billions of years to complete their life-cycles, not millions.

Now try this

target
G-D

1. Write these stages in the life cycle in order: main sequence, white dwarf, red giant, nebula. **(1 mark)**

2. What pulls the gas in a nebula together? **(1 mark)**

target
D-C

3. Explain why a white dwarf begins to cool down. **(2 marks)**

Theories about the Universe

Different theories

There are two different theories about the Universe.

The Big Bang theory says that the whole Universe started out as a tiny particle about 13.5 billion years ago. The Universe expanded from this point in space. The Universe is still expanding today.

The Steady State theory says that the Universe has always existed. It is expanding, and new matter is being created as it expands.

Red-shift

If a vehicle with a siren goes past you, you can hear the sound change. The movement of the siren changes the frequency and wavelength of the sound waves that you hear.

The black lines can be seen in the light from the Sun.

Sun ★

distant galaxy

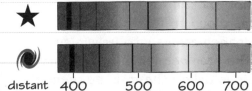

400   500   600   700

When a distant galaxy is moving away, the black lines in its spectrum shift towards the red end.

A similar effect happens with light. Black lines in the spectrum of light from a star are moved closer to the red end of the spectrum if the star is moving away from us. This is called red-shift.

Light from distant galaxies shows red-shift. The galaxies are moving away from us. This shows that the Universe is expanding. Red-shift supports both theories, as both theories say that the Universe is expanding.

Worked example

Describe the cosmic microwave background radiation (CMB) and explain why the Big Bang theory is the currently accepted model for the beginning of the Universe.

You need to be able to describe the cosmic microwave background radiation for your exam.

The cosmic microwave background radiation is detected by radio telescopes and comes from all over the sky. The Big Bang theory says that this radiation was released at the beginning of the Universe.

Red-shift supports both the Big Bang and the Steady State theories, but the CMB only supports the Big Bang theory. The Big Bang theory is accepted because it has the most evidence supporting it.

Now try this

target D-C

1. Which theory or theories say that the Universe is expanding? **(1 mark)**

2. The light from a galaxy is red-shifted. What does this tell us about the movement of the galaxy? **(1 mark)**

3. Which theory or theories are supported by:
   (a) the red-shift of galaxies? **(1 mark)**
   (b) the CMB? **(1 mark)**

Infrasound

Humans can hear sounds with frequencies between 20 Hz and 20 000 Hz.

Other frequencies

Sounds with frequencies lower than 20 Hz are called infrasound. Sounds with frequencies higher than 20 000 Hz are called ultrasound (see the next page).

'Ultra' and 'infra' have the same meanings for electromagnetic waves. Ultraviolet light has higher frequencies than visible violet light, and infrared light has lower frequencies than visible red light.

Students often confuse infrasound and ultrasound waves with other kinds of waves. Infrasound and ultrasound are sound waves. They just have different frequencies and wavelengths from the sounds that humans can hear.

Animals

Infrasound can travel further through air, water or the ground than sounds with higher frequencies. Some animals, such as whales and elephants, use infrasound for communication. They can make infrasound, and they can also hear it.

Worked example

Humans cannot hear infrasound. Explain how humans can use infrasound to study animals, and why this is important.

Scientists can use special instruments to detect sounds the animals are making. This allows scientists to follow the movements of the animals. Information about where animals are moving can help scientists to study them and to recommend how animals can be protected.

Meteors and volcanoes

Meteors burn up as they travel through the Earth's atmosphere. ➤ As they pass through the air they produce infrasound waves. ➤ Scientists can detect these waves. ➤ They work out how many meteors enter the atmosphere and the paths they follow.

Erupting volcanoes produce infrasound. → The infrasound is detected by instruments all over the Earth. → Scientists detect volcanoes erupting in remote areas. → Governments can send help to people in the area.

Scientists learn more about volcanoes and how they erupt.

Now try this

target
G-D

1. State the difference between infrasound and 'normal' sound. **(1 mark)**

2. (a) Describe two ways in which humans use infrasound. **(2 marks)**

   (b) Choose one of your answers to part (a), and explain why that use is important. **(1 mark)**

Ultrasound

Animals

Animals such as bats and dolphins can make and detect ultrasounds. They use these sounds to communicate with one another.

Scans

Ultrasound waves are used to make images of the inside of the body. Ultrasounds are not harmful, so it is safe to use them to scan foetuses (unborn babies). The ultrasound waves are sent into the woman's body, and some of the sound is reflected each time it meets a different type of tissue. The scanner detects the echoes and a computer uses the information to make a picture.

Sonar

Sonar uses pulses of ultrasound to find the depth of water beneath a ship. The sonar equipment measures the time between sending the sound and detecting its echo. This time is used to calculate the depth of the water, using this equation:

distance = speed × time (see page 73)

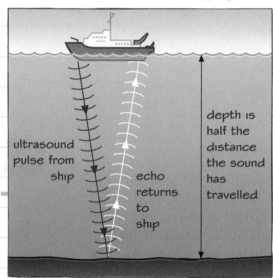

ultrasound pulse from ship

echo returns to ship

depth is half the distance the sound has travelled

Worked example

A ship detects an echo 5 seconds after it has sent out a sonar pulse. Sound travels at 1500 m/s in sea water. How deep is the water?

distance = speed × time
= 1500 m/s × 5 sec
= 7500 m

Depth of water = $\frac{7500 \text{ m}}{2}$
= 3750 m

Be careful with the units. If the speed is in metres per second, the time must be in seconds.

Remember that the depth of the water is *half* the distance the ultrasound has travelled.

Now try this

target D-C

1. Describe how an ultrasound scan produces a picture of a foetus. Include the following words in your answer: reflected, echo, detect, picture.

   (4 marks)

2. A sonar signal is sent out from a boat. The echo is received 0.2 s later. The sound has travelled 280 m. What is the speed of sound in water? Use the formula speed = distance ÷ time.

   (2 marks)

Seismic waves

P waves and S waves

Seismic waves can be caused by earthquakes or explosions. Seismic waves can be P waves or S waves. P waves are longitudinal waves, and S waves are transverse waves. P waves travel faster than S waves.

You can remember the different types of wave using this method:

P waves push and pull the rock as they pass, so they are longitudinal.

S waves move the rocks side to side as they pass, so they are transverse.

P waves make the rocks move in the same direction as the wave is travelling.

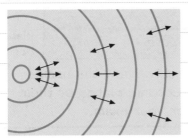

S waves make the rocks move at right angles to the direction the wave is travelling

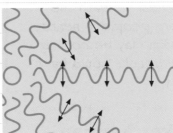

Investigating the Earth

Like all waves, seismic waves can be reflected or refracted (see page 70) when they meet different materials. The Earth is made of different materials in the core, mantle and crust. Seismic waves are reflected and refracted at the boundaries between these different layers.

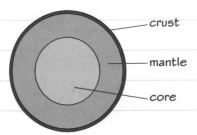

crust — mantle — core

Worked example

Explain how seismic waves can be used to find out where an earthquake happened.

P waves are primary waves, so they arrive first. S waves are secondary waves, so they arrive second.

Seismic waves spread out in all directions from the point where the earthquake happens, and the waves are detected by seismometers. P waves travel faster than S waves, so they are detected first. The greater the distance between the earthquake and seismometer, the greater the difference in arrival times. Scientists use the difference in the arrival times of the P waves and S waves to work out the distance from each seismometer to the place where the earthquake happened. Distances from at least three seismometers in different places are used to work out where the earthquake happened.

Now try this

target G-D

1. State two differences between S waves and P waves. **(2 marks)**

2. Name the three layers of the Earth, starting with the outermost layer. **(1 mark)**

target D-C

3. Describe how the position of an earthquake is located using P and S waves. **(3 marks)**

Predicting earthquakes

Earthquakes cause a lot of damage, and people can be killed by falling buildings. If an earthquake happens beneath the sea it can cause a huge wave called a tsunami. Tsunamis kill thousands of people and destroy buildings near the coast.

Scientists can give people warnings about tsunamis. Seismometers are used to find the location of an earthquake. If the earthquake happened beneath the sea then they can warn people in nearby countries that a tsunami may be coming. People living near the coasts could have several hours warning.

Tectonic plates

The outermost layer of the Earth is divided into sections called tectonic plates. The plates move slowly, driven by convection currents in the Earth's mantle.

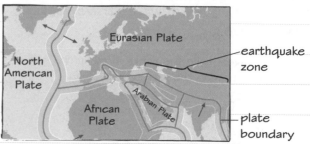

You don't need to know the names of different tectonic plates or their boundaries for your exam.

How earthquakes happen

| Tectonic plates move slowly driven by convection currents in mantle | → | No gaps between plates so their edges slide past each other | → | Friction between plates means they don't slide smoothly | → | Forces build up until part of the plate breaks | → | Plates move with a sudden jerk |

EARTHQUAKE

Worked example

Give two reasons why scientists cannot predict when an earthquake will happen.

1. They don't know how big the forces acting on the tectonic plates are.

2. They don't know the amount of friction on the plates or how strong they are so they can't predict when they will break.

The question asks for two reasons. It is a good idea to number your answer to make sure that you have written down two different reasons.

Where do earthquakes happen?

Earthquakes happen at the boundaries between tectonic plates. This means scientists can predict where an earthquake might take place, even if they can't predict when.

Now try this

1. (a) Which part of the Earth is divided into tectonic plates? **(1 mark)**

   (b) Explain why the plates move. **(2 marks)**

2. (a) What causes earthquakes? **(1 mark)**

   (b) What causes tsunamis? **(2 marks)**

3. Explain why scientists cannot predict when an earthquake will happen.

   (2 marks)

This part of the question has two marks, so you need to link two ideas in your answer. Think about *what* makes the plates move, and *where* this happens in the Earth.

Physics extended writing 2

The Sun was formed about 5 billion years ago when gravity pulled a cloud of gas together. The Earth formed about half a billion years after that. The Earth will last for about another 5 billion years before it is destroyed by the Sun. The Sun will eventually become a white dwarf.

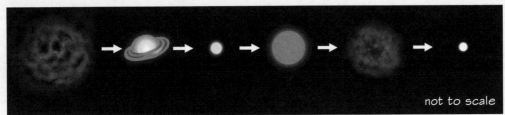

not to scale

Explain how the Sun formed, and why it will eventually destroy the Earth. **(6 marks)**

Sample answer 1

Gravity pulled the cloud of gas together to make the Sun. The Sun shines because of nuclear reactions. When the nuclear reactions stop the Sun will explode and destroy the Earth.

This is a basic answer. The first sentence is correct, but the question says this so there are no marks for it. The second sentence correctly mentions nuclear reactions, but the statement that the Sun will explode is not correct.

Sample answer 2

When gravity pulled the gas together it got hot and the pressure increased. Nuclear reactions started and the Sun began to shine. The Sun is a main sequence star. When the nuclear fuel is used up the Sun will swell up to become a red giant. It will be big enough to reach the Earth and destroy it.

This is a good answer, but it could be even better. The student could have said that the nuclear reactions fuse hydrogen nuclei together to form helium, and it is when the hydrogen fuel is used up that the red giant forms.

Take some time to think about your answer before you start writing, so you can put down your ideas in a sensible order.

Writing your answer in correct English is very important, so check your spelling. Try to use the correct scientific words whenever you can.

1. Galileo (1564–1642) was the first person to use a telescope to study the sky in detail. Among his discoveries were mountains on the Moon and the moons of Jupiter.

   The way astronomers work today is very different from the way that Galileo worked. Describe some ways in which modern astronomy is different from Galileo's observations. **(6 marks)**

Physics extended writing 3

Worked example

The Earth's crust is divided into sections called tectonic plates. The existence of these plates was first suggested when scientists discovered that there are lines of mountains running down the plate boundary in the middle of the Atlantic Ocean and beneath the other oceans.

Explain how ultrasound waves were used to help scientists to discover the boundaries between the tectonic plates beneath the ocean. **(6 marks)**

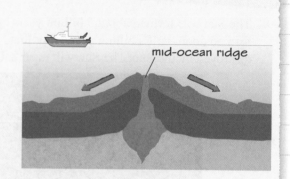

mid-ocean ridge

Sample answer 1

Ultrasound waves bounce off the sea bed. The machine hears the waves coming back and finds how deep the water is and so you can find mountains.

This is a basic answer. The student understands that ultrasound waves are used to find the depth of water and knows something about how this works. However there is a lot of detail missing.

As well as putting in more detail, this student needs to use correct scientific language such as 'sonar', and 'reflect' instead of 'bounce'.

Sample answer 2

Ultrasound waves are used by sonar systems to find the depth of water. Sonar equipment sends out a pulse of ultrasound waves. These waves are reflected by the sea bed. The sonar equipment detects the echo, and measures the time between sending the pulse and receiving the echo. The distance the pulse has travelled is worked out from the length of time and from the speed of sound in water.

A ship travelling across the ocean sending out sonar pulses will detect changes in the depth of the sea. If the sea suddenly gets shallower, there might be mountains on the sea bed. If lots of ships do this, we can get a map of the sea bed.

This is a good answer. It starts by explaining how sonar works and how sonar systems are used to find the depth of water, and then it explains how a map of the oceans can be made. This is a sensible way of organising the answer. It could be turned into an excellent answer by explaining *how* the depth is worked out from the speed and time.

Now try this

1. Seismic waves travel through the Earth. Describe the similarities and differences between S waves and P waves.

   (6 marks)

Answers describing similarities and differences can be presented as a table or a set of bullet points. But make sure you write enough in each bullet point or part of the table – proper sentences are best.

Renewable resources

Electricity is not a source of energy. It has to be generated using renewable or non-renewable energy resources.

Renewable resources

Renewable energy resources are resources that are easily replaced.

For example, solar energy can be used in special power stations to generate electricity. Solar cells can also turn energy from the Sun into electricity directly.

Wind can be used to turn turbines, which power generators. Waves can generate electricity in floating generators or in small power stations built on the coast.

Tides can be used to generate electricity using water flowing through barrages, or by using underwater turbines.

Hydroelectricity is generated by flowing rivers or water falling from a dam in the hills. Geothermal energy uses heat underground to turn water to steam, and the steam drives turbines. Electricity can also be generated by burning food waste called biomass, and biofuels can also be used as an alternative to petrol (see page 60).

These resources depend on the weather, so they are not available all the time. Solar energy is more abundant in countries sunnier than the UK!

These renewable resources are available all the time (except for tides). However, there are not many suitable places to use these in the UK.

Worked example

Explain how electricity can be made using energy in the tides.

A tidal barrage can be built across an estuary to trap water as the tide goes out. The trapped water then flows through turbines to make them spin. The turbines turn a generator that generates electricity. Turbines can also be put under the sea, where strong tidal currents flow.

You need to remember key words such as tidal barrage (a dam built across a river or estuary) and turbine (a machine that spins when wind or water flows past it).

Advantages and disadvantages of renewable resources

- ✓ Generating electricity using renewable resources does not usually cause pollution.
- ✓ There are no fuel costs.
- ✗ Although there are no fuel costs, it does cost money to build the machinery to generate electricity.
- ✗ Many people think that wind turbines spoil the view.

- ✗ The reservoirs used for hydroelectricity flood valleys, and tidal barrages change the environment in river estuaries. Both of these change habitats and can harm wildlife.
- ✗ Most forms of renewable energy are not available all the time.

Now try this

target
G-D

1. Write down two forms of renewable energy that:
   (a) depend on the weather   **(b)** do not depend on the weather.   **(4 marks)**

2. State two advantages of using renewable resources to generate electricity.   **(2 marks)**

Non-renewable resources

Non-renewable resources include fossil fuels (coal, oil and natural gas) and nuclear fuel. Most electricity in the UK is generated from non-renewable resources.

Advantages and disadvantages of fossil fuels

✓ Electricity from power stations is available all the time (unlike electricity from renewable resources).

✓ At present, generating electricity using fossil fuels is cheaper than using renewable resources (although fossil fuels will become more expensive as they begin to run out).

✗ Burning fossil fuels releases carbon dioxide (which is contributing to climate change) and sulfur dioxide (which causes acid rain).

✗ Extracting and transporting fossil fuels causes pollution and can change landscapes.

EXAM ALERT!

Give details if you are answering a question about fossil fuels. Don't just say 'causes pollution', but say which gases are released.

Students have struggled with this topic in recent exams – **be prepared!**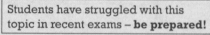

You need to remember the polluting gases produced by burning fossil fuels.

Nuclear power

✓ Nuclear power stations do not release carbon dioxide or other polluting gases.

✗ The uranium used as nuclear fuel will run out one day.

✗ Nuclear power stations produce radioactive waste, which stays radioactive for millions of years. This must be sealed into glass or concrete and buried so that the radioactivity cannot damage the environment.

✗ An accident in a nuclear power station could affect thousands or even millions of people. Nuclear power stations must be safe, making them much more expensive to build than fossil fuelled power stations.

✗ Nuclear power stations are very expensive to decommission (dismantle) at the end of their life.

✗ Many people are worried about the possibilities of an accident in a nuclear power station, and do not want to use nuclear energy.

Now try this

target G-D

1. State two advantages of using fossil fuels to generate electricity. **(2 marks)**

2. Name two polluting gases released by fossil-fuelled power stations. **(2 marks)**

target D-C

3. Explain one advantage that nuclear power stations have over fossil-fuelled power stations, and one disadvantage. **(2 marks)**

Generating electricity

Inducing a current

If you move part of a loop of wire in a magnetic field, an electric current will flow in the wire. This is called electromagnetic induction, and the current is an induced current.

You can get the same effect by keeping the wire still and moving the magnet.

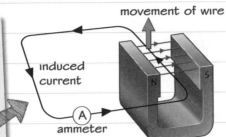

movement of wire

induced current

A ammeter

You can change the direction of the current by:

- changing the direction of motion of the wire
- changing the direction of the magnetic field.

You can increase the size of the current by:

- moving the wire faster
- using stronger magnets
- using more loops of wire, so there is more wire moving through the magnetic field.

Generators

This diagram shows a simple generator. The generators in power stations work in a similar way to the one in the diagram. However, they need to use very strong magnetic fields, so they usually use electromagnets instead of permanent magnets.

Permanent magnets produce a magnetic field. The stronger the magnetic field, the greater the current.

A coil is wound on an iron core. The many turns of wire and the iron core increase the size of the current.

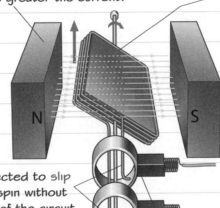

The ends of the coil are connected to slip rings. These allow the coil to spin without twisting the wires to the rest of the circuit.

Induced alternating current (a.c.)

Carbon brushes press on the slip rings to make electrical contact with the rest of the circuit.

An alternating current changes direction many times each second. Generators produce alternating current because each side of the coil goes up through the magnetic field and then comes down again. This induces a current in one direction then in the opposite direction.

Direct current (produced by batteries) always flows in the same direction.

Now try this

target G-D

1. How will the induced current in a straight wire (top diagram) change if:
   (a) the wire is moved more slowly?   **(1 mark)**
   (b) the wire is moved downwards?   **(1 mark)**

2. Describe the difference between alternating and direct current.   **(2 marks)**

target D-C

3. Suggest three ways in which the current produced by the generator could be increased.
   (3 marks)

Transmitting electricity

The National Grid is the system of wires that transmit electricity from power stations to the places where the electricity is used. Electricity is transmitted at high voltage. This improves the efficiency because less energy is wasted as heat in the transmission lines.

Transformers

Transformers are used to change the size of the voltage in an alternating current. Increasing the voltage reduces the current.

Remember: step-up transformers increase the voltage before electricity is transmitted. Step-down transformers reduce it to safer voltages again before it goes into homes.

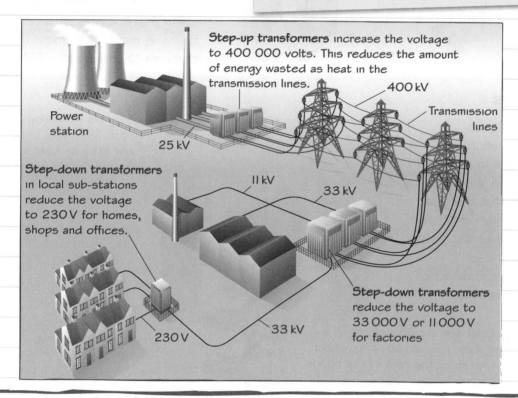

Step-up transformers increase the voltage to 400 000 volts. This reduces the amount of energy wasted as heat in the transmission lines.

400 kV

Transmission lines

Power station

25 kV

Step-down transformers in local sub-stations reduce the voltage to 230 V for homes, shops and offices.

11 kV

33 kV

Step-down transformers reduce the voltage to 33 000 V or 11 000 V for factories

230 V

33 kV

Worked example

Electricity is supplied to homes at 230 V. This voltage is enough to seriously harm you and could even kill you. Explain why the electricity in transmission lines is even more dangerous.

Anyone touching a transmission wire could be killed because electricity is transmitted at very high voltages. You could also be killed if a kite string or carbon fishing pole comes into contact with a transmission wire, because the electricity can flow through the string or fishing pole.

Now try this

1. What is the National Grid? **(1 mark)**

2. Which kind of transformer (step-up or step-down) is used to change:
   (a) 33 kV to 230 V? **(1 mark)**
   (b) 25 kV to 400 kV? **(1 mark)**

3. Explain why electricity is sent around the National Grid at high voltages. **(2 marks)**

Electrical power

Current and voltage

Electricity is a flow of charged particles. Current is the amount of charge flowing past a point each second. Voltage is like an electrical pressure – it measures the amount of energy transferred by a current.

Power

The power of an appliance is the amount of energy it transfers every second. Energy is measured in joules (J) and power is measured in watts (W).

EXAM ALERT!

Students often get power and energy confused. Power is *how fast* energy is being transferred. Remember that 1 watt is 1 joule being transferred every second.

Students have struggled with this topic in recent exams – **be prepared!** Results Plus

---

Calculating power

Power can be calculated using this equation:

$$P = \frac{E}{t}$$

P = power (watt, W)
E = energy (joule, J)
t = time (second, s)

The power of an electrical appliance can also be calculated using the current and the voltage:

$$P = I \times V$$

P = power (watt, W)
I = current (amp, A)
V = voltage (volt, V)

Worked example

The current in a torch bulb is 0.2 A. The voltage across the bulb is 6 V. What is the power of the bulb?

power = current × voltage
= 0.2 A × 6 V
= 1.2 W

You do not need to memorise the equations, as they will be given to you in an exam. But you *do* need to be able to choose the correct equation to use and remember the correct units for the different quantities.

Finding the power

This circuit can be used to find the power of an appliance.

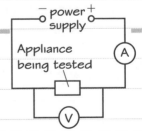

Now try this

target G-D

1. A light bulb transfers 600 J of energy in 10 seconds. Calculate its power and give the unit. **(3 marks)**

2. A 1000 W kettle is plugged into the 230 V mains supply. Calculate the current in the kettle and give the unit. Use the equation current = power ÷ voltage. **(3 marks)**

target D-C

3. A machine transfers 500 J of energy in one minute. Calculate its power and give the unit. **(4 marks)**

Paying for electricity

Power ratings

The energy transferred by an appliance depends on its power and the time it is switched on for. The power rating of an appliance tells you how much energy it uses each second.

Some appliances transfer a lot of energy. Their power ratings are often given in kilowatts. 1 kilowatt (kW) = 1000 W

Units for energy

In most science work we use the joule as the unit for energy. Electricity companies use a much larger unit for energy, the kilowatt-hour (kWh). This is the amount of energy transferred by a 1 kW appliance in 1 hour.

> Don't get kilowatts and kilowatt-hours mixed up! Remember that kilowatts are a unit for power, and kilowatt-hours are a unit for energy.

Worked example

It takes 3 minutes to boil a 2 kW kettle. Electricity costs 15 p/kWh. How much does it cost to boil the kettle?

cost (p) = power (kilowatt, kW) × time (hour, h)
          × cost of 1 kW h (p/kWh)

The time must be in hours.

3 minutes = 3/60 hours
        = 0.05 hours

cost   = 2 kW × 0.05 h × 15p/kWh
         = 1.5p

> Be careful with your units! If you are using the equations for calculating power on page 95 then the power must be in watts and the time in seconds.
>
> If you are calculating the cost of electricity, the power must be in kilowatts and the time in hours.

Check your answer to see if it is sensible:

• An electricity bill for 3 months shouldn't be more than around £200 (or 20 000 p).

• The cost of running an appliance for a few hours shouldn't be more than a few pounds.

• The cost of running an appliance for a few minutes shouldn't be more than a few pence.

If you get a very large number, check that you have used the correct units – the power should be in kW and the time should be in hours.

Now try this

1. For each of these units, say whether it is a unit for power or for energy:
   (a) kilowatt   **(1 mark)**
   (b) joule   **(1 mark)**
   (c) kilowatt-hour.   **(1 mark)**

2. A 2 kW electric fire is switched on for 2 hours. Calculate the cost if the price of electricity is 16p/kW h.   **(3 marks)**

3. A 100 watt (0.1 kW) bulb is switched on for 6 hours. Electricity costs 14p per unit. Calculate the cost.   **(2 marks)**

Reducing energy use

Using less energy saves us money. It also helps the environment because most forms of energy we use to generate electricity result in carbon dioxide being added to the atmosphere.

Using less energy

Use efficient light bulbs:

Old light bulb:
10 W of light output
100 W of energy input

Modern light bulb:
10 W of light output
20 W of energy input

Use microwave ovens:

- use less energy than a normal oven
- cook food more quickly
- but some people don't like them because the food does not go brown.

Insulate homes:

Insulation reduces the amount of energy lost from homes, and reduces heating bills.

Payback times

Although you will save some money by using a low-energy appliance or insulating your home, you need to spend money to buy the appliance or the insulation. The payback time is the time it takes to save the amount of money you had to spend to start with.

$$\text{payback time} = \frac{\text{cost of energy-saving method}}{\text{savings per year}}$$

Worked example

It costs a homeowner £75 to have extra insulation added to their loft. They should save about £25 per year on their energy bills. What is the payback time?

$$\text{payback time} = \frac{£75}{£25 \text{ per year}}$$

$$= 3 \text{ years}$$

Making decisions

The most cost-efficient method is the one with the shortest payback time. This is the one that will give you the biggest savings for each pound you spend.

Cost isn't always the only thing to consider when buying new appliances. For example, you might want a new fridge because your current one is too small.

Now try this

target G-D

1. A homeowner is trying to decide whether to have her loft insulated or to replace her fridge with a lower-energy model. What information does she need to help her to make her decision?
(2 marks)

target D-C

2. It costs £2 000 to fit double glazing to a small house. The savings per year are £150. What is the payback time? **(2 marks)**

Energy transfers

Energy is never created or destroyed. The total energy before an energy transfer is exactly the same as the total energy afterwards. The energy has just been changed into one or more different forms. This is the law of conservation of energy.

Forms of energy

Energy can be changed from one form to another. The forms of energy are:

- thermal (heat energy)
- light
- sound
- electrical
- kinetic (movement)
- chemical (energy stored in food, fuel, etc.)
- nuclear (energy stored within atoms)
- elastic potential (energy stored in stretched springs, etc.)
- gravitational potential (energy stored in objects in high positions).

Energy transfer chains

This is an energy transfer chain for a battery operated radio. It shows the different forms of energy in the radio.

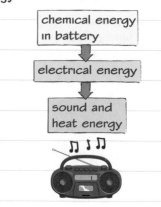

chemical energy in battery

↓

electrical energy

↓

sound and heat energy

Worked example

The diagram shows the energy transfers in a kettle.

(a) Fill in the missing value.

(b) Calculate how much energy is wasted when the kettle is boiled.

(a)

Heat energy to kettle and surroundings

28 kJ

Electrical energy 210 kJ

Sound energy 2 kJ

Heat energy to water 180 kJ

(b) 28 kJ + 2 kJ = 30 kJ

In an energy transfer diagram the width of each arrow represents the amount of each type of energy. You may be asked to fill in missing numbers on diagrams like this, or to explain what they show.

The total amount of useful and wasted energy transferred is the same as the energy that was supplied to the kettle.

210 − 180 − 2 = 28

The heat energy transferred to the water in the kettle is useful energy. The rest of the energy is wasted energy.

Now try this

target
G-D

1. Draw a flow chart to show the energy changes when you lift a box onto a high shelf. Start with the chemical energy stored in your muscles. **(2 marks)**

2. Look at the energy transfer diagram for the kettle. What form of energy is most of the wasted energy in the kettle? **(1 mark)**

target
D-C

3. A kettle uses 375 kJ of electrical energy to heat some water. 300 kJ of energy ends up as useful thermal (heat) energy in the water. Calculate the amount of energy wasted. **(2 marks)**

Efficiency

Efficiency

All machines waste some of the energy they transfer. Most machines waste energy as heat energy. The efficiency of a machine is a way of saying how good it is at transferring energy into useful forms.

A very efficient machine has an efficiency that is nearly 100%. The higher the efficiency, the better the machine is at transferring energy to useful forms.

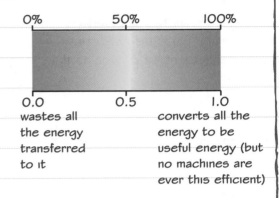

0.0 wastes all the energy transferred to it

1.0 converts all the energy to be useful energy (but no machines are ever this efficient)

Worked example

What is the efficiency of this television?

60 J of heat energy — wasted energy

100 J of electrical energy

12 J of sound energy — useful energy

28 J of light energy

$$efficiency = \frac{useful\ energy\ transferred\ by\ the\ machine}{total\ energy\ supplied\ to\ the\ machine} \times 100\%$$

Efficiency does not have units.

Total useful energy = 12 J + 28 J
= 40 J

$$efficiency = \frac{40\ J}{100\ J} \times 100\%$$

= 40%

No machine is ever 100% efficient. If you calculate an efficiency greater than 100% you have done something wrong!

Now try this

target **G-D**

1. What is the wasted form of energy from light bulbs (lamps)? **(1 mark)**

target **D-C**

2. An old style filament lamp uses 60 J of electrical energy, and transfers 6 J of this to light energy.

   (a) How much energy is wasted? **(1 mark)**

   (b) What is the efficiency of the lamp? **(2 marks)**

60 J of electrical energy each second

6 J of light energy each second

The Earth's temperature

Energy balance

Any object that has a constant temperature must be absorbing the same amount of power as it is radiating.

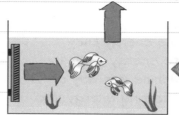

The warm water loses heat to its surroundings.

power in = power out
temperature constant

The water is heated by an electric heater.

If the power absorbed is greater than the power radiated, it will warm up.

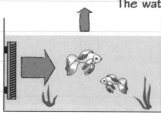

The heater is switched to a higher power setting. Power in is greater than power out → temperature rises

If the power absorbed is less than the power radiated, it will cool down.

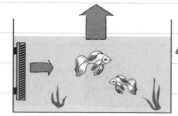

The heater is switched to a lower power setting. Power out is greater than power in → temperature falls

Remember that power is the amount of energy transferred each second.

Worked example

Peter investigates the factors that affect the amount of radiation absorbed by different coloured objects. He uses cans of water painted black, grey and white, and stands them in the sun. Explain which can will have the hottest water after 5 minutes.

The water in the black can will be the hottest, because black surfaces absorb more thermal energy than paler surfaces.

Black surfaces absorb more thermal energy than white surfaces. Black surfaces also radiate more thermal energy than white ones.

The Earth

The Earth is warmed by absorbing energy radiated by the Sun. The warm Earth radiates radiation into space.

If the power absorbed from the Sun is the same as the power radiated, the Earth stays at the same temperature.

Some gases in the atmosphere act as 'greenhouse gases'. They absorb some energy radiating from the Earth and stop it being radiated away into space. This means that the amount of radiation emitted by the Earth is now less than the amount absorbed. The Earth warms up.

Now try this

target G-D

1. The air in a room is at a constant temperature. There is a 2000 W electric fire heating the room.
   (a) State the power that the room is radiating to its surroundings. **(1 mark)**
   (b) Explain how you worked out your answer. **(2 marks)**

target D-C

2. A fish tank without a lid contains a small heater. The temperature in the tank reaches a steady value. Explain what will happen to the temperature of the water in the fish tank if you now put a lid on the tank. **(3 marks)**

Physics extended writing 4

Worked example

The efficiency of a kettle is the amount of energy used to heat the water inside it, compared with the total energy supplied to the kettle. A joulemeter can be used to measure the amount. Sue investigates which of these kettles is the most efficient. Describe how she should carry out her investigation, and how she can make her test fair. **(6 marks)**

If you are asked to describe a method, remember to describe what to do, what measurements to make and what variables must be controlled.

Sample answer 1

She should boil the same amount of water in each kettle. She needs to use the joulemeter to find out how much energy it uses. She should start with cold water.

This is a basic answer. It describes one variable that needs to be kept the same. The description is not very clear. It uses the information given in the question to describe how Sue can measure the amount of energy used by each kettle. It does not say how to control the variables, and is not written in a very logical order.

Sample answer 2

Sue can compare the efficiencies of the three kettles by measuring the amount of energy it takes to heat the same amount of water in each one.

She needs to control the amount of water used, and its starting and finishing temperatures. She should use a measuring cylinder to put the same volume of water into each kettle. She should use a thermometer to measure the starting temperature of the water. She should connect the kettle to the joulemeter and switch it on. She should switch off when the water has gone up by 50°C. She should repeat this for the other kettles.

Her results will be more reliable if she repeats the measurements and takes an average of the results for each kettle, but she should allow each kettle to cool down again before repeating the test. The kettle that takes the least amount of energy to heat the water by 50°C is the most efficient.

This is an excellent answer because it explains which variables need to be controlled and how to control them. It describes what should be done in a sensible order, and also explains how to make the results more reliable. This answer also says how the results will show which kettle is the most efficient. This is a better method than just finding out how long it takes the water to boil. It is not easy to tell the exact moment when water starts to boil.

Now try this

1. The table shows the costs and savings for some different ways of reducing energy bills.

   Discuss how the different methods will help to reduce energy bills, and which change the homeowner should choose to do first. **(6 marks)**

Change to house	Cost to install	Savings per year
double glazing	£4000	£200
insulate hot water tank	£50	£10
cavity wall insulation	£300	£100
loft insulation	£160	£140
solar panels to heat water	£3000	£50

Physics Extended Writing 5

Worked example

The Earth receives energy all the time from the Sun. The Earth also sends energy back into space.

Sam set up an experiment to model the Sun and the Earth. When the heater is switched on the sphere eventually comes to a steady temperature of 20 °C.

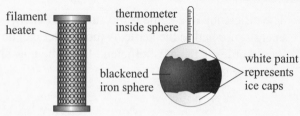

Sam wants to use some spheres like this to model the effect of changes in the amount of ice at the poles. He thinks that:
- each sphere will reach a constant temperature
- the constant temperature will be different for each sphere.

Explain how Sam could use this model to illustrate the effects he expects to get. **(6 marks)**

Sample answer 1

The white paint is clouds and ice. If he paints it white it will be more clouds. He can paint it all black to show no ice. It will be hotter with all black, because black absorbs more heat.

This is a basic answer. It does not explain why the model Earth comes to a steady temperature. The statements are correct, but there is not enough detail.

Sample answer 2

The heater warms the sphere and its temperature rises. As it gets hotter the sphere emits more energy, until the amounts it is absorbing and emitting each second are the same. This is why it will reach a constant temperature.

The white paint on the sphere represents clouds and ice. Sam can model more ice at the poles by having a sphere with more white paint, or he can model the ice caps melting by painting more of it black.

White surfaces do not absorb as much radiation as black ones. When more of the sphere is white it will reflect more of the energy from the heater so it will not get as hot. Its final temperature will be less than 20 °C. When it is all black it will absorb more energy and its final steady temperature will be higher than 20 °C.

This is an excellent answer. It includes correct scientific words such as 'absorb', 'emit' and 'reflect'. The answer could have related the results of the model to the Earth, by saying that perhaps more ice at the poles would cool the Earth.

Now try this

1. A solar power station uses mirrors to focus sunlight onto a central furnace. Water turns to steam, and the steam is used to spin turbines, which turn the generators.

   There are advantages and disadvantages of using solar power stations and hydroelectric stations. Compare the use of these two sources of energy to generate electricity in the UK. **(6 marks)**

Practical work 1

Questions on practical work

Your Edexcel Science course includes suggestions for a lot of different investigations. By the time you sit your exams you will have completed a Controlled Assessment, based on one or more of these investigations. But you could also be asked questions about any of these practicals in the exam.

Questions based on practical work could include:
- writing a method for an investigation
- explaining how to carry out a fair test
- drawing a graph to show some results
- writing a conclusion based on results given in the exam paper
- evaluating a method or a conclusion.

Worked example

A student is investigating the effectiveness of different indigestion remedies. He is using a pH meter to find out how the pH of hydrochloric acid changes when he adds one dose of each indigestion remedy.

Explain how the student can control three different variables to make the test fair.

(1) He should use the same volume of acid each time, by measuring it into the beaker using a measuring cylinder.

(2) He should use the same concentration of acid each time. He can do this by using acid from the same bottle each time.

(3) He should leave each indigestion remedy in the acid for the same length of time before taking the pH reading. He can use a stopclock to tell him when to measure the pH.

This is a good answer, because the student has explained *how* to control each variable.

Other variables that could have been mentioned in this answer include keeping the temperature the same (as temperature can affect the rate of reactions), and stirring the mixture in the same way each time.

Other questions on planning

Other questions on the planning part of a practical could include asking you to:
- describe a method
- explain the apparatus needed.

Say why you need each piece of apparatus. Remember to include apparatus you may need to control variables.

You must describe a method in the correct order. It may help to jot down some ideas in a blank space on your exam paper to help you to get your ideas in order.

If the question asks you to explain the method, remember to say why each step is needed.

Practical work 2

Dealing with evidence

Worked example

The graph shows the results of an investigation to find out how the current flowing through an appliance changes when the voltage is changed. Complete the graph by drawing a line of best fit.

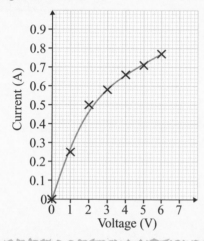

A result that does not fit the pattern is an anomalous result. The student has probably made a mistake when measuring or recording the result for 2 V.

Do not include anomalous results when you are working out means, or when you are drawing lines or curves of best fit.

EXAM ALERT!

This is a good answer, because the student has drawn a smooth curve through most of the points. Do not join each of the points using straight lines. Try to include as many points as possible on your curve, but ignore any that are obviously not following the pattern of most of your results.

Students have struggled with questions similar to this - **be prepared!**   ResultsPlus

Conclusions and evaluations

Worked example

A student investigating current and voltage in an appliance had the following hypothesis:

'The current will increase when the voltage increases'.

Look at the graph of their results (above).
(a) Write a conclusion for this investigation.
(b) Evaluate the quality of the conclusion.

(a) The graph shows that the current increases when the voltage increases. My hypothesis was correct.

(b) The points all lie close to a smooth curve, so there were probably not many errors in the measurements. The quality of the data could be improved by taking several measurements at each voltage and finding means (averages) of the results.

Only one appliance was tested, so the conclusion really only applies to this appliance. Several different appliances would need to be tested before we could test the hypothesis properly and know whether this conclusion applies to all appliances.

This would be a better answer if the conclusion described the shape of the graph in more detail. The graph is a curve, which shows that the increase in current for each step in voltage gets less as the voltage gets higher.

Stating whether or not the hypothesis is correct is good. But this would be better if the answer pointed out that the current is not proportional to the voltage in this appliance. Proportional means that the current doubles if the voltage doubles.

Taking at least three readings for each point and finding a mean is almost always a good way of improving the quality of data. To calculate a mean, add up all the results for each point and then divide by the number of results.

Answers

You will find some advice next to some of the answers. This is written in italics. It is not part of the mark scheme but just gives you a little more information.

Biology answers

3. Classification

1. kingdom, phylum, class, order, family, genus, species **(1)**
2. **(a)** Plants have chlorophyll **(1)** but fungi do not. **(1)**
   (b) A protoctist has a cell nucleus **(1)** but a prokaryote does not. **(1)**

4. Vertebrates and invertebrates

1. fish, amphibians, reptiles, birds, mammals **(5)**
2. oviparous – lays eggs **(1)**
   viviparous – live births **(1)**
   poikilotherm – varying body temperature **(1)**
   homeotherm – controlled body temperature **(1)**

5. Species

1. Any one from: publish papers in scientific journals, tell other scientists at conferences. **(1)**
2. Some organisms from closely related species can interbreed and produce fertile hybrid offspring. **(1)**
   Some organisms divide in two, so don't breed with another individual, and so we cannot be sure if they are the same species or not. **(1)**
3. Different individuals of the same species look different. **(1)**

6. Variation

1. To help identify organisms. **(1)**
2. Picking out a distinguishable feature of each organism **(max. 2)** correctly leading to each organism **(max. 2)**

7. Reasons for variety

1. Any two from: no light, high pressure, very high temperatures, low oxygen concentration, high concentration of minerals, acidic. **(2)**
2. **(a)** discontinuous **(1)**
   (b) discontinuous **(1)**
   (c) by genes only **(1)**
3. Thick fur is insulation against the cold **(1)**, white colour is camouflage against the snow. **(1)**

8. Evolution

1. DNA studies **(1)**   antibiotic resistance in bacteria **(1)**
2. Natural selection is how individuals that are better adapted to the environment are more likely than other individuals to survive and pass on their adaptations to their offspring. **(1)**
   Evolution is the gradual change in characteristics of a species over time. **(1)**
3. If you don't use antibiotics then you don't select for bacteria that are resistant **(1)**, so the variation in bacteria for resistance won't change and there will be no evolution. **(1)**

9. Genes

1. **(a)** An allele is an alternative form of a gene. **(1)**
   (b) A gene is a short piece of DNA that codes for a characteristic. **(1)**
2. **(a)** It is heterozygous **(1)** because it has one of each type of allele. **(1)**
   (b) Purple flowers, **(1)** because purple is dominant over white. **(1)**

10. Explaining inheritance

1. **(a)** genotype Bb **(1)**   phenotype brown **(1)**
   (b)

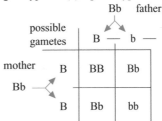

   (**1 mark** for setting out the gametes and genotypes correctly, **1 mark** for completing the phenotypes correctly)
   (c) genotype ratio: 1 BB : 2 Bb : 1 bb **(1)**
   phenotype ratio: 3 brown : 1 black **(1)**

11. Genetic disorders

1. **(a)** Any one genetic disorder, such as sickle cell disease, or cystic fibrosis. **(1)**
   (b) For sickle cell disease, any two from: short of breath, tired easily, painful joints, blocked blood vessel causing death. For cystic fibrosis, any two from: thick sticky mucus, many lung infections, loss of weight. **(2)**
2. A diagram that shows who in a family **(1)** has a particular characteristic. **(1)**
3. **(a)** Gill and Harry **(1)**
   (b) Their daughter Mia has inherited two copies of the faulty allele, one from each of her parents. **(1)** But neither Gill nor Harry has the disease so they must each have one copy of the faulty allele/be carriers. **(1)**

12 and 13. Biology extended writing 1 and 2

Answers can be found on pages 110 and 111.

14. Homeostasis

1. inside **(1)**   the same/steady **(1)** (*or equivalent*)
2. If the body contains too much water, you produce lots of watery urine to get rid of lots of water. **(1)** If your body contains too little water, you produce only a little concentrated urine so you don't lose much water. **(1)**
3. Blood glucose increases **(1)** as glucose is taken into the body after digestion. **(1)**

15. Thermoregulation

1. temperature **(1)**
2. hypothalamus **(1)**
3. **(a)** Any one from: more blood flows near the skin surface, you make more sweat, body hair lies flat. **(1)**
   (b) Any one from: less blood flows near the skin surface, no sweat is made, body hair is raised by erector muscles. **(1)**

16. Sensitivity

1. brain **(1)**   spinal cord **(1)**
2. **(a)** It collects impulses from receptor cells and carries them to the central nervous system/spinal cord/brain. **(1)**
   (b) It carries nerve impulses from neurones in the central nervous system/spinal cord/brain to effector organs. **(1)** *You could say muscle or gland cells here, instead of effector organs, but effector organs is better because it is more general.*
   (c) central nervous system **(1)** *This is better than saying either brain or spinal cord, as it means both of these.*

17. Responding to stimuli

1. Touch different parts of the skin with two pointers set at different distances apart **(1)**. In sensitive areas, the person will be able to say that there are two pointers instead of one when they are closer together than in areas that are less sensitive. **(1)**

2. The reflex arc is very short/contains very few neurones **(1)** so the response is very quick. **(1)**

3. When the impulse reaches the end of the sensory neurone it causes neurotransmitter chemical to be released **(1)** into the gap in the synapse. **(1)** The chemical crosses the gap and causes a new electrical impulse in the next neurone. **(1)**

18. Hormones

1. **(a)** chemical message **(1)**
   (b) the blood **(1)**   target organ **(1)**

2. It causes blood glucose concentration to fall **(1)** and causes muscle and liver cells to take glucose out of the blood **(1)**

3. **(a)** It is released into the blood by the pancreas **(1)** when an increase in blood glucose concentration is detected. **(1)**
   (b) The pancreas releases less insulin into the blood **(1)** as blood glucose concentration falls. **(1)**

19. Diabetes

1. No insulin produced by pancreas. **(1)** *Remember to say that it is the pancreas that should produce insulin.*

2. BMI = $100/(1.8)^2$ = 100/3.24 = 30.9. **(1)** for putting the numbers into the equation correctly, **(1)** for correct answer. This is greater than 30 so he is obese. **(1)**

3. Muscle cells use more energy during exercise than at rest, **(1)** so this will take more glucose out of the blood and help to reduce blood glucose concentration. **(1)**

20. Plant hormones

1. **(a)** Plant shoots grow towards **(1)** light. **(1)** *You must include the word 'grow' in your answer to get the first mark, because this is a growth response.*
   (b) Positive **(1)** because roots grow towards gravity. **(1)**

2. auxins **(1)**   gibberellins **(1)**

3. When a shoot gets light from one side, auxin from the tip moves to the shaded side of the shoot. **(1)** This causes cells on the shaded side to grow longer than those on the light side, **(1)** so the shoot will curve as it grows so the tip is pointing to the light. **(1)**

21. Biology extended writing 3

Answers can be found on page 111.

22. Effects of drugs

1. **(a)** alcohol/any other depressant **(1)**
   (b) Changes the way you respond to a stimulus such as vision, sound or the perception of time. **(1)**

2. reduces feeling of pain (by blocking pain reception by brain) **(1)** makes you feel sleepy **(1)**

3. **(a)** reduces reaction time **(1)**
   (b) It is a stimulant **(1)** so you respond more quickly. **(1)**

23. The damage caused by smoking

1. **(a)** tar **(1)**
   (b) carbon monoxide **(1)**

2. **(a)** nicotine **(1)**
   (b) It is addictive, **(1)** which makes it difficult to live without it. **(1)**

3. Tobacco smoke contains carcinogens in tar that can cause cancers of the lungs, **(1)** so smokers are more likely to develop lung cancer than non-smokers. **(1)**

24. The effects of alcohol

1. **(a)** Any one from: blurred vision, vomiting (or any other suitable answer). **(1)**
   (b) Any one from: liver cirrhosis, brain damage. **(1)**

2. **(a)** depressant **(1)**
   (b) Depressants slow down your reactions **(1)**. This is dangerous when driving as it increases the chance of an accident. **(1)**

25. Ethics and transplants

1. A decision about what is right or wrong/fair or unfair. **(1)**

2. This can increase the number of organs available for transplant. **(1)**

3. Hospitals may have to choose between patients, because there are not enough organs **(1)** so they have to make a fair choice between patients. **(1)**

26. Pathogens and infection

1. Any one from: bacteria, fungi, viruses, protoctists. **(1)**

2. A pathogen is an organism that causes disease. **(1)** A vector is an organism that helps to spread a pathogen from an infected person to another person. **(1)**

3. in water e.g. cholera **(1)**   by air e.g. flu **(1)**   by direct contact e.g. athlete's foot **(1)**   in body fluids e.g. HIV **(1)**   by vector e.g. malaria or dysentery **(1)** *It is a good idea to learn the names of all the diseases and the vectors.*

27. Antiseptics and antibiotics

1. Any one from: mucus in nose and throat, cilia in nose and throat, skin **(1)** and any one of: hydrochloric acid in stomach, lysozymes in tears. **(1)**

2. **(a)** antifungal cream **(1)**
   (b) Because it will kill the fungus that is causing the athlete's foot infection. **(1)**

3. **(a)** B **(1)**
   (b) Because the area clear of bacteria is much bigger than around A. **(1)**

28. Interdependence and food webs

1. **(a)** Pyramid of similar shape to the one on page 28, with three levels (grass at bottom, mice in middle and owls at top), **(1)** with the bottom bar widest, middle bar smaller and top bar shortest. **(1)**
   (b) There is not enough energy in the biomass of the owls for organisms at another trophic level to get all the energy they need to grow and reproduce. **(1)**

29. Parasites and mutualists

1. b **(1)**

2. **(a)** The flea pierces the skin to feed on the host's blood. **(1)**
   (b) The host/human is harmed while the flea benefits. **(1)**

3. Both organisms benefit from the relationship. **(1)**

30. Pollution

1. A pollutant is something that harms the environment or the organisms that live in it. **(1)**

2. Human population is continuing to increase **(1)**, so we release more pollutants as we grow more food or make more products. **(1)**

3. Eutrophication increases the rate of growth of plants and algae. **(1)** This can cause plants lower in the water to die. **(1)** Bacteria feeding on the dead plants take oxygen from the water. **(1)** There is not enough oxygen for fish so they die. **(1)** *Watch out: eutrophication does not kill fish directly. They die because of lack of oxygen caused by the bacteria taking more oxygen from the water.*

31. Pollution indicators

1. **(a)** no pollution **(1)**
   (b) pollution **(1)**
   (c) no pollution **(1)**

2. **(a)** Stonefly larvae only grow well in water with lots of oxygen. **(1)**
   (b) Sludgeworms can grow in water that has little oxygen, which is when the water is polluted. **(1)**
   (c) Blackspot fungus is killed by air pollution, so the presence of the fungus on roses shows there is no air pollution. **(1)**

3. To reduce the amount of new resources we use. **(1)** *This includes the fossil fuels used to generate electricity for making the products.* To reduce the amount of waste we dump in landfill tips or incinerate/burn. **(1)**

32. The carbon cycle

1. carbon dioxide **(1)**
2. combustion – releases carbon from compounds in fossil fuels as carbon dioxide gas into the air
   photosynthesis – changes carbon dioxide gas into carbon compounds in living organisms
   respiration – releases carbon from compounds in living organisms as carbon dioxide gas into the air. **(1)** for getting one right, **(2)** for getting all three.
3. Decomposers break down/decay dead organisms **(1)** and release carbon back into the air as carbon dioxide from respiration. **(1)**

33 and 34. Biology extended writing 4 and 5

Answers can be found on page 111.

Chemistry answers

35. The early atmosphere

1. **(a)** carbon dioxide **(1)**   water vapour **(1)**
   (b) volcanoes **(1)**
2. Water vapour in the atmosphere condensed **(1)** when the Earth cooled down. **(1)**

36. A changing atmosphere

1. It has decreased. **(1)**
2. **(a)** calcium carbonate **(1)**
   (b) Marine organisms fall to the sea bed when the creatures die. **(1)** Sediments build up and become compressed **(1)** and the calcium carbonate turns into limestone. **(1)** *Remember that if there are three marks for a question, you need to make three points in your answer.*
3. Oxygen is produced by photosynthesis **(1)** and organisms that carry out photosynthesis did not evolve until about 1 billion years ago **(1)**.

37. The atmosphere today

1. nitrogen **(1)**
2. **(a)** Any two from: burning fossil fuels, farming, deforestation. **(2)**
   (b) sulfur dioxide **(1)**
3. Any two from the following: volcanoes can add sulfur dioxide **(1)** and carbon dioxide, **(1)** plants can absorb carbon dioxide **(1)** and add oxygen. **(1)**

38. Rocks and their formation

1. **(a)** limestone **(1)**   chalk **(1)**
   (b) granite **(1)**   basalt **(1)**
2. The liquid rock that formed granite cooled down more slowly than the liquid rock that formed basalt **(1)** so the crystals had time to grow bigger. **(1)**
3. They are not made of interlocking crystals. **(1)** *Just saying that sedimentary rocks are softer is not a very good explanation.*

39. Limestone and its uses

1. Any three from: roads, buildings, glass, cement, concrete. **(3)**
2. Compounds breaking down **(1)** when they are heated. **(1)**
3. **(a)** Any one from: providing more jobs, workers at the quarry spending more money in local shops. **(1)** *Providing important raw materials and helping the UK economy are economic advantages, but they are not really* local *advantages.*
   (b) Any one from: producing dust, producing noise, destroying habitats, spoiling the scenery. **(1)** *Producing dust and noise could also be considered to be social disadvantages, as they affect the people living nearby.*

40. Compounds and formulae

1. calcium **(1)**   carbon **(1)**   oxygen **(1)**
2. **(a)** **(1)**   **(b)** **(1)**
3. **(a)** element **(1)**   **(b)** compound **(1)**

41. Chemical reactions

1. **(a)** copper carbonate → copper oxide + carbon dioxide **(2)**
   (b) copper carbonate **(1)**
2. 3 g **(1)**

42. Reactions of calcium compounds

1. It turns cloudy (or milky) **(1)**
2. They can be used to neutralise **(1)** acid soils. **(1)**
3. There is fizzing (or bubbles), **(1)** steam is seen **(1)** and the calcium oxide crumbles to a white powder. **(1)**

43. Chemistry extended writing 1

Answers can be found on page 111.

44. Indigestion

1. to help with digestion **(1)**   to kill bacteria **(1)**
2. too much acid in the stomach **(1)**
3. salt **(1)**   water **(1)**
4. 7 **(1)**

45. Neutralisation

1. oxides **(1)**   hydroxides **(1)**   carbonates **(1)**
2. Acids can be dangerous if they are not used properly. **(1)** The hazard symbols show what the hazards are **(1)** and allow people to look up the precautions they should take when using them. **(1)** *There are three marks for this question, so a simple answer such as 'acids are dangerous' is not going to get you full marks! If there are 3 marks, you need three ideas or points in your answer.*
3. **(a)** magnesium oxide + sulfuric acid → magnesium sulfate + water **(1)** for the two compounds on the left of the arrow. It doesn't matter which way round you wrote them. **(1)** for magnesium sulfate, and **(1)** for water.
   (b) copper carbonate + hydrochloric acid **(1)** → copper chloride **(1)** + carbon dioxide + water **(1)** for putting both carbon dioxide and water

46. The importance of chlorine

1. hydrogen **(1)**   chlorine **(1)**
2. Any two from: making bleach, making PVC, disinfectant. **(2)**
3. The electrolysis of sea water produces chlorine, **(1)** which is a toxic gas. **(1)** Ventilating the laboratory makes sure the gas does not build up to dangerous levels. **(1)**

47. The electrolysis of water

1. **(a)** hydrogen and oxygen **(1)**
   (b) hydrogen and chlorine **(1)**
2. **(a)** oxygen **(1)**
   (b) hydrogen **(1)**

48. Ores

1. gold, silver, platinum **(1)**
2. Magnesium costs more to extract. **(1)** Magnesium is more reactive than tin **(1)** and electrolysis is more expensive than heating with carbon. **(1)**
3. **(a)** by heating with carbon **(1)**
   (b) tin oxide + carbon **(1)** → tin + carbon dioxide **(1)**

49. Oxidation and reduction

1. **(a)** reduction **(1)**
   (b) oxidation **(1)**
2. Lead is more resistant to corrosion **(1)** because it is less reactive than zinc. **(1)**
3. copper + oxygen **(1)** → copper oxide **(1)**

50. Recycling metals

1. For some metals it costs more to collect, sort and transport them **(1)** than is saved by recycling them. **(1)**

...eases sulfur dioxide into the atmosphere when it is ...) but this does not happen when lead is recycled. **(1)** ...y is needed to recycle lead than to extract it, **(1)** so less .. dioxide is released from burning fossil fuels. **(1)**

.. Properties of metals

1. **(a)** It does not corrode easily. **(1)**
   (b) It has a low density. **(1)**
   (c) It is a very good conductor of electricity. **(1)**
2. In iron, layers of atoms can slide over each other **(1)** when there is a force on the metal. **(1)** In steel there are atoms of different sizes **(1)** which stop the layers sliding when they are pushed. **(1)**

52 and 53. Chemistry extended writing 2 and 3

Answers can be found on page 111.

54. Crude oil

1. B **(1)**   C **(1)**
2. **(a)** fractional **(1)** distillation **(1)**
   (b) The fractions are more useful **(1)** than the crude oil mixture. **(1)**

55. Crude oil fractions

1. petrol **(1)**   diesel oil **(1)**
2. fuel oil **(1)**
3. **(a)** gases **(1)**
   (b) bitumen **(1)**
   (c) gases **(1)**

56. Combustion

1. **(a)** ethane **(1)** + oxygen **(1)** → carbon dioxide **(1)** + water **(1)**
   (b) ethane **(1)**
2. **(a)** Bubble the gas **(1)** through limewater. **(1)**
   (b) The limewater will turn milky. **(1)** *You can say milky or cloudy.*

57. Incomplete combustion

1. **(a)** water **(1)**
   (b) carbon, carbon dioxide, carbon monoxide **(2)** if you get all three, **(1)** if you only get two of them
2. It is toxic (or poisonous) **(1)** because it reduces the amount of oxygen that the blood can carry. **(1)**
3. Any one from: may build up and cause fires, may cause lung disease, makes buildings dirty. **(1)**

58. Acid rain

1. **(a)** carbon dioxide **(1)**   sulfur dioxide **(1)**
   (b) sulfur dioxide **(1)**
2. It can make lakes/rivers/soils acidic, **(1)** it damages trees, **(1)** it speeds up the weathering of buildings/statues. **(1)**

59. Climate change

1. methane **(1)**   carbon dioxide **(1)**   water vapour **(1)**
2. Any two from: we are putting more carbon dioxide into the atmosphere **(1)** by burning fossil fuels, **(1)** which is making the Earth warmer. **(1)**
3. Seeding the oceans with iron. **(1)** Converting carbon dioxide from power stations into hydrocarbons to use as fuels. **(1)**

60. Biofuels

1. A fuel made from living organisms. **(1)** *You may get a mark for just putting 'ethanol', but ethanol is just one example of a biofuel. The answer given here is a better answer.*
2. More plants can be grown to make more fuel, **(1)** so biofuels will never run out. **(1)**
3. Advantage: any one from: renewable, add less carbon dioxide to the atmosphere overall when they are burnt. **(1)**
   Disadvantage: use land that could be used for growing food. **(1)**

61. Choosing fuels

1. **(a)** petrol, kerosene, diesel oil **(1)** *You could also say fuel oil here.*
   (b) methane **(1)**
2. Any two from: petrol is a liquid, **(1)** so it is easier to transport/use in an engine. **(1)** Coal is a solid so it is difficult to use automatically. **(1)**

62. Alkanes

1. methane **(1)**   ethane **(1)**   propane **(1)**
2. hydrogen **(1)**   carbon **(1)**
3. C_3H_8 **(1)**

63. Alkenes

1.

   (1) for correct number of carbon atoms, **(1)** for correct number of hydrogen atoms, **(1)** for joining them up correctly and including a double bond.
2. **(a)** They both contain two carbon atoms **(1)** and they both have hydrogen atoms joined to the carbon atoms. **(1)** *You could also say that they are both hydrocarbons for the 2nd mark.*
   (b) Ethene has a double bond between the two carbon atoms, but ethane only has a single bond; **(1)** ethane has six hydrogen atoms but ethane has four hydrogen atoms. **(1)** *If you are asked to describe differences, you need to say something about both of the things you are comparing.*
3. **(a)** There would be no colour change **(1)** because ethane does not contain a double bond. **(1)** *You would also get the 2nd mark if you said that ethane is saturated, or that it does not react with bromine.*
   (b) The colour of the bromine water would disappear, **(1)** because it reacts with unsaturated compounds (or compounds containing a double bond). **(1)**

64. Cracking

1. To make them into smaller, **(1)** more useful molecules. **(1)**
2. Any one from: wear eye protection (safety glasses or safety goggles), be careful when handling hot apparatus, remove the delivery tube from the water before stopping the heating. **(1)** *You are not expected to know all of these. Generally, if the experiment involves heating or using substances such as acids or alkalis, one safety precaution is always to wear eye protection.*
3. Shake a sample of the gas with bromine water. **(1)** If the sample contains unsaturated molecules the mixture will change from orange to colourless. **(1)**

65. Polymerisation

1. **(a)** polymer **(1)**
   (b) monomer **(1)**
2. **(a)** poly(ethene) **(1)**
   (b) PVC **(1)**
3. good insulator **(1)**

66. Problems with polymers

1. **(a)** Microbes **(1)** do not break polymers down. **(1)**
   (b) Polymers in landfill sites will remain there for a very long time **(1)** and we are running out of landfill sites. **(1)**
2. Burning polymers releases toxic gases. **(1)**
3. Recycling means using the material to make new objects **(1)** so the material is not thrown away/burnt/put into landfill. **(1)**

67 and 68. Chemistry extended writing 4 and 5

Answers can be found on page 111.

Physics answers

69. The Solar System

1. The geocentric model has the Earth in the centre with the Sun and planets orbiting around it, **(1)** and the heliocentric model has the Sun in the centre with the Earth and planets orbiting around it **(1)**.
2. **(a)** He discovered that Jupiter has moons orbiting around it. **(1)**
   (b) The geocentric model said that everything in the sky moved around (orbited) the Earth, **(1)** but moons orbiting Jupiter was evidence that some things moved around (orbited) a different body. **(1)**

70. Reflection and refraction

1. refraction **(1)**
2. The distance between the centre of the lens **(1)** and the point to which parallel **(1)** rays of light are brought together. **(1)**
3. Use the converging lens to focus parallel rays of light **(1)** such as from a distant scene **(1)** onto a screen. **(1)** Measure the distance between the centre of the lens and the screen. **(1)** This is the focal length of the lens.

71. Telescopes

1. **(a)** reflecting telescope **(1)**
   (b) simple telescope (refracting telescope) **(1)**
2. **(a)** eyepiece lens **(1)**
   (b) eyepiece lens **(1)**

72. Waves

1. **(a)** metres (or m) **(1)**
   (b) metres per second (or m/s) **(1)**
   (c) hertz (or Hz) **(1)**
2. amplitude **(1)**   wavelength **(1)**   for correct shape **(1)**

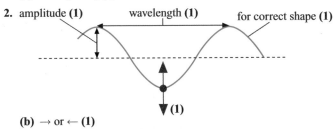

   (1)

   (b) → or ← **(1)**

73. Wave equations

1. $v = f \times \lambda$
   $v = 100\ \text{Hz} \times 3.3\ \text{m}$ **(1)** for putting the correct numbers into the equation
   $= 330\ \text{m/s}$ **(1)** for the number, **(1)** for the correct unit
2. $v = \dfrac{x}{t}$
   $v = 1500\ \text{m}/60\ \text{s}$ **(1)** for putting the correct numbers into the equation
   $= 25\ \text{m/s}$ **(1)** for the number, **(1)** for the correct unit

74. Beyond the visible

1. **(a)** red **(1)**
   (b) violet **(1)**
2. The temperature rise would be smaller **(1)** than that for violet light **(1)** because the temperature rise decreases from the red to the violet end of the visible spectrum. **(1)**

75. The electromagnetic spectrum

1. ultraviolet **(1)**   X-rays **(1)**   gamma rays **(1)**
2. **(a)** gamma rays **(1)**
   (b) radio waves **(1)**
3. They are all transverse waves. **(1)** They all travel at the same speed in a vacuum. **(1)**

76. Electromagnetic dangers

1. They transfer less energy **(1)** because they have lower frequencies. **(1)**

2. **(a)** ultraviolet, X-rays, gamma rays **(1)**
   (b) microwaves, infrared **(1)**
   (c) ultraviolet **(1)**

77. Using electromagnetic radiation

There are many possible correct answers to these questions. These are just some of the points that could get marks.

1. **(a)** Microwaves are used to heat food from the inside. **(1)** Infrared is used to heat food from the outside, in grills and toasters. **(1)**
   (b) Infrared is used in cameras to track people at night, and in burglar alarm sensors to detect people. **(1)** Ultraviolet is used to detect special security markings on valuable items or banknotes. **(1)** X-rays are used to look inside luggage at airports. **(1)**
   (c) X-rays are used to look inside the body. **(1)** Gamma rays are used to detect and treat cancer, and to sterilise medical equipment. **(1)**
2. radio waves – to communicate with ships, aeroplanes and satellites **(1)**
   microwaves – for mobile phones and to communicate with satellites **(1)**
   infrared – in optical fibres **(1)**

78. Ionising radiation

1. **(a)** gamma rays **(1)**
   (b) alpha, beta **(1)**
2. **(a)** Ionising radiation can ionise atoms in the body. **(1)** The ions are reactive and can damage DNA. **(1)** This can lead to cancer **(1)** or mutate/kill cells **(1)**.
   (b) Hazard symbols warn about the dangers **(1)** so people can follow safe-working procedures **(1)**.

79. Physics extended writing 1

Answers can be found on page 111.

80. The Universe

1. The Sun and everything orbiting it. **(1)**
2. moon **(1)**
3. Sirius **(1)**

81. Exploring the Universe

1. Any three from: infrared, ultraviolet, X-rays, gamma rays. **(3)**
2. The Earth's atmosphere absorbs X-rays, **(1)** so an X-ray telescope on the ground would not detect anything (or, so the X-ray telescope must be above the atmosphere). **(1)**

82. Alien life?

1. water **(1)**, oxygen **(1)**
2. Any two from: take close-up images, test soil samples, investigate below the surface. **(2)**
3. The soil may contain microscopic organisms **(1)** or substances that are only made by living organisms. **(1)**

83. Life-cycles of stars

1. nebula, main sequence, red giant, white dwarf **(1)**
2. gravity **(1)**
3. A white dwarf star has used up all its nuclear fuel **(1)** so it is no longer being heated. **(1)**

84. Theories about the Universe

1. Big Bang and Steady State **(1)** (for both)
2. It is moving away from us. **(1)**
3. **(a)** both the Big Bang and Steady State theories **(1)**
   (b) Big Bang **(1)**

85. Infrasound

1. Infrasound has frequencies lower than 20 Hz. **(1)** *It would also be correct to say they have longer wavelengths.*

2. **(a)** Any two from: they detect infrasound made by animals **(1)** to follow their movements. **(1)** They detect infrasound made by volcanoes **(1)** to find out when they are erupting. **(1)** They detect infrasounds made as meteors go through the air **(1)** so they can find out when meteors go through the atmosphere. **(1)**

(b) For animals: learn more about the animals/work out how protect them **(1)**

For volcanoes: learn more about volcanoes/allow help to be sent to areas affected by volcanoes **(1)**

For meteors: learn more about meteors/find out how many meteors enter the atmosphere **(1)**

86. Ultrasound

1. Ultrasound waves are sent into the woman's body, **(1)** they are reflected by different layers of tissue, **(1)** the echoes are detected by the scanner, **(1)** a computer builds the information into a picture. **(1)**

2. speed = 280 m/0.2 s **(1)**
   = 1400 m/s **(1)**

87. Seismic waves

1. S waves are transverse and P waves are longitudinal. **(1)** P waves travel faster than S waves. **(1)**

2. crust, mantle, core **(1)**

3. Seismic waves are detected by seismometers. **(1)** The distance from the earthquake to each seismometer is worked out from the difference in the arrival times of P waves and S waves. **(1)** The distances of the earthquake from many different seismometers are used to work out the location. **(1)**

88. Predicting earthquakes

1. **(a)** The outermost layer. **(1)** *It is not the crust, as tectonic plates include part of the mantle as well.*

   (b) Convection currents **(1)** in the mantle **(1)** make the plates move.

2. **(a)** Plates moving past each other. **(1)**

   (b) An earthquake **(1)** that happens beneath the sea. **(1)**

3. There are lots of factors that affect when an earthquake will happen **(1)** and scientists cannot measure any of them accurately. **(1)**

89 and 90. Physics extended writing 2 and 3

Answers can be found on page 111.

91. Renewable resources

1. **(a)** Any two from: wind, waves, solar. **(2)**

   (b) Any two from: tidal, hydroelectricity, geothermal. **(2)**

2. Any two from: they do not pollute the atmosphere, they do not have any fuel costs, they are easily replaced. **(2)**

92. Non-renewable resources

1. They are available all the time **(1)** and they are cheaper than using renewable resources. **(1)**

2. carbon dioxide **(1)**   sulfur dioxide **(1)**

3. Nuclear fuelled power stations are better than fossil fuelled ones because they do not release any polluting gases. **(1)** Nuclear power stations are worse because they are more expensive to build and decommission. **(1)** *You could also have said that people worry about nuclear accidents.*

93. Generating electricity

1. **(a)** It will be less. **(1)**

   (b) It will flow in the opposite direction. **(1)**

2. Direct current always flows in the same direction. **(1)** Alternating current changes direction. **(1)** *If you are asked to compare two things, you need to mention both in your answer.*

3. Put more turns of wire on the coil, **(1)** spin the coil faster, **(1)** use stronger magnets. **(1)**

94. Transmitting electricity

1. The wires that carry electricity around the country **(1)**.

2. **(a)** step-down **(1)** *Remember that 33 kV is 33 000 V*

   (b) step-up **(1)**

3. Less energy is wasted than if it is sent at lower voltages **(1)** because the current is lower **(1)**.

95. Electrical power

1. power = 600 J/10 s **(1)** = 60 **(1)** W **(1)**

2. current = 1000 W/230 V **(1)** = 4.35 **(1)** A **(1)**

3. 1 minute = 60 seconds **(1)**
   power = 500 J/60 s **(1)** = 8.33 **(1)** W **(1)**

96. Paying for electricity

1. **(a)** power **(1)**

   (b) energy **(1)**

   (c) energy **(1)**

2. cost = 2 kW × 2 h × 16 p/kWh **(1)** = 64 **(1)** p **(1)**

3. cost = 0.1 kW × 6 h × 14 p/kWh **(1)** = 8.4 p **(1)** *When you are calculating costs, the power must always be in kW.*

97. Reducing energy use

1. The costs of the insulation and the fridge, **(1)** and how much money each one will save her each year. **(1)**

2. payback time = £2000/£150 per year = 13.3 years **(2)**

98. Energy transfers

1. chemical energy → kinetic energy **(1)** → gravitational potential energy **(1)**

2. thermal (heat) energy in the kettle and the surroundings **(1)**

3. wasted energy = 375 kJ – 300 kJ **(1)**
   = 75 kJ **(1)**

99. Efficiency

1. thermal (heat) **(1)**

2. **(a)** 60 J – 6 J = 54 J **(1)**

   (b) efficiency = 6 J/60 J × 100% **(1)** = 10% **(1)**

100. The Earth's temperature

1. **(a)** 2000 W

   (b) If the temperature is staying the same the power in from the fire **(1)** must be the same as the power out (to surroundings). **(1)**

2. The lid will reduce the power transferred to the surroundings. **(1)** There will be more power being absorbed by the water than being transferred from it **(1)** and the temperature will rise. **(1)**

101 and 102. Physics extended writing 4 and 5

Answers can be found on page 111.

Extended writing answers

Below you will find a list of points which will help you to check how well you have answered each Extended writing question. Your actual answer should be written in complete sentences, it will contain lots of detail and will link the points into a logical order. A full answer will contain most of the points listed but does not have to include all of them and may include other valid statements. You are more likely to be awarded a higher mark if you use correct scientific language and are careful with your spelling and grammar.

12. Biology extended writing 1

Polar bears live in cold climates; they have thick, white fur; wide feet; fat layer under the skin; small ears; the thick fur helps to insulate the bear and stops heat escaping; white fur helps to camouflage it so that it can hunt more efficiently; wide feet give it greater friction and stop it slipping on the ice; small ears mean a smaller surface area and less heat will escape.

13. Biology extended writing 2

Chromosomes are found in the nucleus; chromosomes contain genes; chromosomes are found in pairs; chromosomes carry genetic information/chromosomes help to pass on characteristics; the genes have different forms called alleles; alleles contain different information for the same characteristic; an example such as a gene for eye colour could contain information for blue eyes or brown eyes; because there are two chromosomes you could have two different alleles for the same characteristic; genes are passed down from parents.

21. Biology extended writing 3

Nerves pass impulses using electricity; nerves are cells; hormones are chemical; hormones are carried in the blood stream; nerves carry impulses to muscles or other nerves, hormones carry effect target organs, the nervous system reacts quickly; the hormone system is slower to respond; information carried by the nervous system is brief and does not have long lasting effects; hormones can cause long-term responses.

33. Biology extended writing 4

Cigarette smoke contains nicotine; cigarette smoke also contains tar; cigarette smoke contains carbon monoxide; tar is a carcinogen; carcinogens cause cancer; smoking increases the risk of developing cancer; nicotine is addictive; carbon monoxide reduces the amount of oxygen that red blood cells can carry; cells in the body need oxygen; smoking can reduce the flow of blood to the heart; smoking is linked with heart disease.

34. Biology extended writing 5

The carbon cycle includes respiration, photosynthesis, combustion of fuels, decomposition, formation of fossil fuels and passing of carbon from one organism to the next (this full list would be worth one than one mark); carbon is found as carbon dioxide in the atmosphere; photosynthesis takes carbon dioxide out of the atmosphere and passes it into plants; carbon passes from plants to animals when the plants are eaten, respiration releases carbon back into the atmosphere as carbon dioxide; when organisms die they decompose and respiration of decomposers releases carbon back into the atmosphere; organisms that do not die may eventually form fossil fuels; burning fossil fuels releases carbon back into the atmosphere as carbon dioxide.

43. Chemistry extended writing 1

The amount of carbon dioxide in the atmosphere has reduced since the early Earth; this started when plants evolved; plants use carbon dioxide in photosynthesis; carbon dioxide dissolved in the oceans, dissolved carbon dioxide helps to form calcium carbonate shells; shells eventually became limestone; carbon dioxide levels today are increasing because humans are burning fossil fuels; carbon dioxide is emitted when volcanoes erupt; carbon dioxide increases when forests are cleared and burned, there are then fewer trees to absorb carbon dioxide in photosynthesis.

52. Chemistry extended writing 2

Chlorine is used to kill microorganisms in water; it is used in manufacturing bleach; it is used in manufacturing plastics; it is toxic, so it can harm people; it kills microorganisms because it is toxic; a large leak could kill people or make them ill; it is safe to use as long as it doesn't leak.

53. Chemistry extended writing 3

Electrolysis decomposes compounds by passing electricity through them; the electrolysis of water produces hydrogen and oxygen; the electrolysis of hydrochloric acid produces hydrogen and chlorine; hydrogen is tested with a lighted splint; if the gas is hydrogen it will explode with a squeaky pop; oxygen is tested with a glowing splint (you will not get a mark for saying 'a blown out splint'); if the gas is oxygen the splint will relight; chlorine is tested with damp blue litmus paper; if the gas is chlorine the paper will turn red and then white.

67. Chemistry extended writing 4

When there is enough air, complete combustion takes place; the anhydrous copper sulfate turns from white to blue, showing that water is being produced; the limewater goes milky, showing that carbon dioxide is being produced; if there is not enough air incomplete combustion takes place; the products are varying amounts of carbon as soot, carbon dioxide, carbon monoxide (which is a toxic gas) and water; the anhydrous copper sulfate still turns from white to blue, and the limewater still turns milky; but there might be a yellow flame and sooty marks on the apparatus.

68. Chemistry extended writing 5

Acid rain is rain that is more acidic than usual; some fossil fuels contain small amounts of sulfur; this forms sulfur dioxide when the fuel burns; this goes into the atmosphere and dissolves in water in the air. Acid rain makes rivers and lakes more acidic, harming wildlife in them; damages trees; speeds up the weathering of rocks and corrosion of metal.

79. Physics extended writing 1

Point the curved mirror towards the thing you wish to observe; it collects light; the mirror is concave; it focuses the light to a point; the plane mirror is placed near the focus; and reflects the light sideways; the plane mirror is small; the plane mirror stops the person's head getting in the way of the light reaching the mirror; the lens is used as a magnifying glass; it refracts the light; so the rays appear to be coming from a larger object; it is a virtual image.

89. Physics extended writing 2

Larger telescopes; these allow dimmer and more distant objects to be seen; modern telescopes can detect parts of the electromagnetic spectrum other than visible light; this allows different kinds of objects in the sky to be seen; astronomers can use photographs to record images; astronomers can use computers to record the images from telescopes; so they do not have to draw what they can see; they can make more accurate star maps; modern astronomers can use computers to help them to analyse the images they record.

90. Physics extended writing 3

This question could be answered using a table, a set of bullet points or by writing two or three short paragraphs.

Both types travel through the earth; both can be detected by seismometers; both are produced by earthquakes and explosions; both can be reflected and refracted; S-waves are transverse but P-waves are longitudinal; in P-waves the particles vibrate in the same direction as the wave is travelling but in S-waves the particles vibrate at right angles to the direction of the wave; P-waves travel faster than S-waves.

101. Physics extended writing 4

This answer could be presented as a table, a set of bullet points or as a paragraph of writing.

Both are renewable resources; neither of them produce pollution; hydroelectricity is available at any time; but solar depends on the weather; both types use up a lot of land (for the reservoir or the mirrors); there are not many sites in the UK suitable for building hydroelectric power stations; the weather in the UK is not sunny enough to make building a solar power station worthwhile.

102. Physics extended writing 5

Double glazing reduces the heat escaping from the house; insulating the hot water tank reduces the heat escaping from the tank; cavity wall insulation reduces heat escaping from the house; loft insulation reduces heat escaping from the house; solar panels mean less energy has to be used for heating water; insulating the hot water tank is the cheapest; a homeowner may do this because they don't have any more money to spend; if they have enough money they should work out which is the most cost effective; the most cost effective is the one with the shortest payback time; this is the amount it costs divided by the savings per year; it shows how many years it takes to save the money spent on the insulation method; loft insulation is the most cost-effective/has the shortest payback time; its payback time is 1.14 years; 20 years for double glazing; 5 years for hot water tank; 3 years for cavity wall insulation; 60 years for solar panels.

Published by Pearson Education Limited, a company incorporated in England and Wales, having its registered office at Edinburgh Gate, Harlow, Essex, CM20 2JE. Registered company number: 872828

www.pearsonschoolsandfecolleges.co.uk

Copies of official specifications for all Edexcel qualifications may be found on the Edexcel website: www.edexcel.com

Text © Pearson Education Limited 2012
Edited by Judith Head and Florence Production Ltd
Typeset by Tech-Set Ltd, Gateshead
Original illustrations © Pearson Education Limited 2012

The rights of Penny Johnson, Sue Kearsey and Damian Riddle to be identified as authors of this work have been asserted by them in accordance with the Copyright, Designs and Patents Act 1988.

First published 2012

18 17 16 15
10 9 8 7 6 5 4

British Library Cataloguing in Publication Data
A catalogue record for this book is available from the British Library

ISBN 978 1 446 90259 2

Acknowledgements
The author and publisher would like to thank the following individuals and organisations for permission to reproduce copyright material:

Figures
Figure 2.6/2 'Relationship between BMI and Type 2 Diabetes', 2006, http://www.cutthewaist.com/impact.html. Reproduced by permission of Cut the Waist Ltd; and Figure 3.3/2 'Relative risk of an accident based on blood alcohol levels' by James Heilman, MD, http://en.wikipedia.org/wiki/File:Relative_risk_of_an_accident_based_on_blood_alcohol_levels_.png. Licensed under the Creative Commons Attribution-Share Alike 3.0 Unported license.

Figure 5.6/1 'Global temperature increase since 1850', www.climatechoices.org.uk/pages/cchange3.htm. Reproduced by permission of Practical Action

Tables
Table 3.2 'Risk Chart for Men (current and never smokers)' in 'Risk of Death by Age, Sex, and Smoking Status in the United States: Putting Health Risks in Context', *Journal of the National Cancer Institute (JNCI)*, Vol. 100, Issue 12, pp. 845–853 (Woloshin, S., Schwartz, L.M. and Welch, H.G. 2008), copyright © 2008, Oxford University Press.

Every effort has been made to contact copyright holders of material reproduced in this book. Any omissions will be rectified in subsequent printings if notice is given to the publishers.

In the writing of this book, no Edexcel examiners authored sections relevant to examination papers for which they have no responsibility.